COMING OF AGE IN KURDISTAN

First Edition 2013

When Mountains Weep

I've had so many great fits of laughter with my friends that sometimes my jaws hurt the next day. But behind the laughs, I hid the pain of my untold stories.

One crisp spring morning, I climbed the big oak tree and tightened the rope to a stout branch over the sheer cliff. Before I put the dangling noose around my neck, I leaned against the tree for my last smoke.

In the distance, the snowy peaks of Gara Mountain emerged behind the skimming black clouds. The magical scent of a fresh rain shower was still in the air. The faint sound of the river below mingled with the chirping of the red-legged partridges the hunters used as bait to attract other birds into the traps of death.

The singing of the partridges added more beauty to the spectacular scene I had selected for my final passage into the other world. The sounds penetrated my thoughts and unearthed some of my long-buried memories. I took the last drag from the cigarette I held between my muddy fingers. As the haze of the smoke disappeared on the breeze, images from my childhood flashed before my eyes.

What to remember!
My first love,
The broken wings of a gentle dove,
My first kiss on her shivering lips,
The first touch from her trembling fingertips

What to remember!
My stolen childhood,
The first slap to my face, in the name of fatherhood,
The first betrayal, in the name of brotherhood,
The first humiliation, for the sake of nationhood,
The first awakening, when they shouted at me,
"Hey, brainless Kurd!"

What to remember!
The first stick, striking down on my shaking hand
From a teacher unable to make me understand.
The first ugly truth: I was born a slave in my own land.
The first tears, for a football I saw in my cousin's hand.
The first shock, visiting the cemetery,
The first puzzle, losing my identity,
The first crime, living in poverty.

What to remember!
The first death, a frozen cat
On my neighbor's doormat.
The first bite from the village dog
In a place where dogs played and men just barked.
The first kick from the village donkey
I had bothered while it was having intercourse,

In a place where donkeys had sex and men just watched.

What to remember!
The first bodily shiver
Watching a furious father
Murder his daughter, a minor,
To restore his lost honor
In a place where men are lauded
And women are slaughtered
For the very same encounter.

Amid all the memories that clashed in my head, I heard my mother's Kurdish lullaby, which echoed through the vast valley. "Sleep, my son, sleep, in this Arabian sand, away from our fathers' land. Sleep, my son, sleep. You may survive to see the day. To our sweet home, we find the way. Smile at your mommy, don't feel sad. Tomorrow you will grow into a lad. And ask for your missing dad. Lull, my darling, lull. Tomorrow you will grow into a man in the mountains of Kurdistan, in a nation without a homeland"

I still remember that distant day when I journeyed out of my neighborhood in Mosul for the first time. My mother held my hand and led me to the corner where a photographer stooped behind his three-legged wooden box. As I posed for my first photo, I wore a wide smile. I was thrilled that I was going to attend school.

After a long walk, my mother and I arrived at an old building where I saw many other children holding their mothers' hands at the school gate. Once we were in the headmistress's room, my mother exchanged a few words in a language I couldn't understand. The only word I could pick out from the conversation was *Hamko*, my name.

Things got even worse the next day. On the way to school, I saw a few children walking barefoot, holding their shoes under their arms. When they arrived at school, they put their shoes on and entered the building.

I went to my classroom on the second floor, where I was surrounded by kids whose language sounded like the chattering of monkeys. I was confused and scurried to the first seat next to the door. As the bell rang, a girl sat beside me and my face flushed with heat.

The teacher entered the classroom holding a book in one hand and a long wooden stick in the other. She wrote something on the chalkboard and read the words aloud, pointing with the stick and asking certain children to repeat after her. When one of the boys failed to repeat the words correctly, she hit him twice on the palms of his hands with the stick and the boy started to cry. I trembled and shrank down in my seat, struggling to control the floodgate of my bladder. I feared she would call on me next.

When class was over, I went outside and wept bitterly, stammering in Kurdish, "I want to go home."

My whole sense of happiness and excitement about attending school faded away as I realized that no one there spoke the way I did and I couldn't understand anyone. Many things happened that day that made little sense to me, but like any six-year old child, I was naturally curious and wondered about those things. Questions floated through my mind, but I had no one to answer them and was hesitant to ask. Among all my ponderings, two were most pressing. *Why did we speak differently in our house, and what was the strange language I was hearing away from home?*

I had grown up in the home of my grandparents, and they pampered me as their first grandson. My grandmother told me that everyone was thrilled when I was born, especially my grandfather. Grandpa had lived his life in utter poverty, so, as Grandma used to say, "He could take your soul from your body before you could snatch the coins from his hands."

But Grandpa was generous on the day of my birth. When the nurse told him that his first grandchild was a boy, he reached into his wallet and handed her his only *dinar.*

Grandpa was an orphan boy with four younger sisters to take care of, which was a disaster in a Kurdish tribal village. A family needed men to carry guns and defend property. Grandpa led a hard, lonely life, wandering among the mountains as an outcast due to his involvement in vendettas between the various Kurdish tribes. The only skill he had learned was how to use a gun.

Grandpa never attended school. The tribal chieftains and sheiks told villagers to avoid educating their children, claiming that education would destroy local customs and traditions. The village elite had good reason to maintain a community shackled by ignorance. To them, education was a dangerous monster that would loosen their grip on naïve peasants who willingly shared half of the year's harvest with them. On the other hand, those same leaders sent their own children to the best schools in the city.

When I returned home from my first frustrating day at school, I heard Grandpa singing a melancholic Kurdish folk song. I ran to him in tears and told him I wasn't going back to school again, because no one spoke Kurdish.

Grandpa stroked my hair with his long, smooth fingers and explained, "Hamko, you should be proud. After all, you're the first boy in our family to go to school."

He then took me by the hand, and led me to his room, saying he wanted to show me something. I watched with curiosity as he reached into a pile of blankets on top of a wooden cupboard and pulled out something wrapped in an oily piece of blue cloth.

Handling it with great care, he unwrapped an old Czech rifle that was taller than I was. My eyes grew wide and my heart pounded in my ears. I'd had a few plastic guns, but this was the first time I'd actually seen a real one.

Looking at the rifle in his hands, Grandpa grew misty-eyed and his voice trembled slightly as he said, "This gun was my best companion for thirty-five years. It was at my shoulder all the time and went with me every place I went—to the mountains, to the orchards, and even to weddings and funerals. The only time I ever put it down was when I was saying my prayers. I even slept with it under my pillow. I used it many times in my life. It didn't matter sometimes who used it or who it was fired at, as long as it brought some bread to the table."

He wiped a few specks of dust from the stock with the sleeve of his white Kurdish *camise*, then looked me in the eye, sighed, and added, "After all these years, I've realized that a gun may protect you from your enemies and put a few coins in your pocket, but I've also learned that carrying a gun is not the way to a better life. So, little Hamko, go to school tomorrow and learn how to read and write, even if it's in the language of your enemies."

At that moment there was a knock on the door, Grandpa quickly rewrapped the rifle and slid it back into its hiding place.

My first year in school passed, and after a rough start, I began to do well as I learned Arabic. One of my favorite classes was drawing. One day, our teacher asked the class to draw a picture of the brave Iraqi army attacking the enemy—Kurdish outlaws in the mountains.

When I put down my crayons, the teacher asked in a firm voice, "Hamko, why are you not drawing?"

"I will not draw what you ask, Teacher, because those men are Peshmargas [those who march to death, Kurdish freedom fighters] and not outlaws," I replied defiantly.

She shouted, "What? Peshmargas! Who taught you that dangerous word?"

Her face was red as she pressed her stick into my chest and yelled, "They are outlaws and they fight our government—and soon the Iraqi army will crush them. They have no leader now that Barzani is finally dead."

I shook my head and said, "My grandfather said Barzani is alive and living with his men in the mountains."

The teacher's anger erupted like a volcano as she grabbed my arm, yanked me from my desk, and marched me to the room of the headmistress. She whispered something into the headmistress's ear as I stood in trembling anticipation. When she had finished, the headmistress's eyebrows raised almost to the top of her forehead. I knew I had made a terrible mistake.

The teacher turned and walked from the room, leaving me alone with the headmistress. The headmistress scowled at me, "Hamko, how dare you use such a disgusting word in my school?"

She opened the small refrigerator by her desk and took out a bottle of water. I thought she was going to offer me a drink, which I really needed because I was sweating out of nervousness. Instead, she told me to stretch out my hands. When I obeyed, she poured the ice-cold water over my hands and hit my wet fingers fiercely and repeatedly with a stick. I started to cry and begged her to stop.

When she had finally finished, she told me to leave school and not return unless I was accompanied by one of my parents. With my hands stinging and tears rolling down my face, I left the building and headed to the house where my parents had rented a room, a few hundred meters from my grandparents' home.

The next day my mother accompanied me to school, where the headmistress warned her that our family must never talk about politics in my presence because it might poison my innocent mind. My mother turned pale as the headmistress threatened to tell the authorities if there was another incident like the one that had gotten me expelled the day before.

As we walked out of the headmistress's office, my mother pressed her hand to my lips and said, "Son, from now on you must hold your tongue. If you don't, you and your grandfather could get us into real trouble."

During the rest of the school year, instead of drawing flowers and birds, the teacher asked us to draw tanks and soldiers flashing *V* signs and waving flags over piles of dead men, women, and children. Every Iraqi textbook featured a photo of the president on the first page—the everlasting historical leader, we were told. In every class, we had to stand and chant, "Long live the president" and "Long live the Arab nation." If it wasn't for the president's wise leadership, we were told, we'd all be homeless, wandering barefoot in the street.

My childhood began with the sound of gunfire and the smell of gunpowder. On Thursdays, the students lined up in the schoolyard to salute the Iraqi flag and listen to a song glorifying the president and his Ba'ath Party. We also had to watch the armed soldier who had been assigned to our school as he fired thirty rounds into the sky—so young children could get used to the clatter of machineguns. Mr. President believed that soft music would turn boys into sissies who would be startled by a sudden honk of a car horn, whereas the pop of gunfire would turn them into great fearless warriors to fight in his glorious wars.

At school, the other boys never called me by my real name. They called me "the Kurd," or sometimes "the brainless Kurd" if they wanted to start a fight. As I passed them, a group of boys would say, "Did you find your brain or are you still looking for it in the mountains?" Then they'd laugh and add, "He can't find his brain because Kurds don't have one!"

Sometimes I was the first to throw a punch, after which they'd knock me down and kick me until I shrank into a little ball to avoid their abuse. Other times I walked away in silence, with my head down.

One day in the schoolyard, a new boy from another class approached me and introduced himself in Kurdish. I was excited to finally have someone to speak to in my native language and to back me up in my fights with the other boys. Abo and I became instant friends.

The next morning, as I was sitting at my desk memorizing a poem, Abo approached me and told me he had learned something interesting. He whispered that while pretending to be asleep he had heard his mother tell his spinster aunt that Arab women never wore underwear.

When I heard that, I smiled, knowing I'd finally have an answer to the derogatory question, "Where is your brain?"

I thought about how to use that precious piece of information—but first we had to confirm it. Abo came up with an idea. We'd stand close to girls in the schoolyard, drop a piece of a broken mirror as close as possible to their feet, and have a look. We actually tried that plan several times, but either the girls left too quickly or the view wasn't clear enough to yield any useful information.

After that, we switched to Plan B and headed for the girls' bathroom. We waited for a girl to go in and then, with a quick kick, we pushed the door open. However, before we could get a look, her shrill scream echoed throughout the corridor. We escaped as fast as we could, but we were soon called to the headmistress's room. I felt weak and my legs trembled as we approached the room. I knocked, then slowly opened the door, pushing Abo ahead of me so he was the first to enter. I shrank behind him.

As she saw us, the headmistress said, "It's you again! You shameless Kurdish boys are a disgrace to our school." She turned toward another two teachers who were sitting in the room and scorned, "It's no wonder their mothers don't teach them manners. How can they have time to teach them anything when all they do is keep the rice cooking and the babies coming? They give birth to a child every nine months. They think it's their national duty so Kurds will become a majority in this country."

Abo and I shook with fear as the headmistress picked up the thickest stick on her table, glared at us, and announced, "The time has come to teach you boys a lesson so you'll start behaving properly in my school."

Abo was the first to feel the sting of her stick, but he tried to be brave, grinding his teeth as he endured several hard slaps to his palms. I could barely hear the slaps over the pounding of my heart. Abo's lower lip quivered and he couldn't stop the tears from rolling down his cheeks, but he never cried out loud. When his ordeal was over, his hands trembled as he wiped away his tears with his shirtsleeve.

Then the headmistress looked at me, waved her stick, and growled, "Hamko, come over here."

I approached her desk slowly and dutifully opened my hands. She raised the stick and brought it down with all her might, but just before it made contact, I pulled my hands away. Her blow landed squarely on the shiny new telephone on her desk, smashing it to pieces. When she realized what had happened, the headmistress no longer focused on my palms. She beat me all over my body and didn't stop until one of the teachers finally intervened and pushed her away from me.

The headmistress screamed, "Both of you get out of here! You're expelled!"

Word had gotten out that the two Kurdish boys were being punished, so a group of boys was waiting outside the headmistress's room when we emerged, but as Abo and I walked out the door, we pretended it hadn't been painful.

One of the boys chided, "Hey, Kurds, did you find your brains?"

Another added, "They don't have brains! They lost them while falling off a rock in their mountains."

Amid the abuse, Abo and I exchanged a glance. Then I said to the Arab boys, "Ask your mothers what happened to their underwear. Did they find them?"

Before anyone could reply, Abo added, "They don't wear underwear. They left it on a camel's head in the desert."

The boys looked at each other in shock at what we had just said and no one said another word to us as we left the building. My body was aching from the beating I had just received, but I'd finally gotten my revenge on those boys.

However, after the ecstasy of my victory faded, I was at a loss as to what I'd tell my family about being expelled a second time. The next day, I left for school at the usual time but couldn't enter the building. I sat near the gate beside a woman who sold *lablabi* sandwiches. She was wearing a traditional black Arab gown and holding a cigarette between her blue-tattooed lips. The ash from her cigarette slowly fell into her old soot-covered pan filled with boiling chickpeas. She stirred the pan with one hand and struggled to keep the swarms of flies at bay with the other.

When she heard the school bell ring, she looked at me and said, "Hey, boy, you'd better hurry. Didn't you hear the bell?"

I told her I couldn't go into the building and I couldn't go home, so I planned to stay right where I was until the school day was over. She smiled at me knowingly and said, "Aha! You must be the underwear boy!"

As I nodded, she said, "Well, then you can help me. I need someone to keep these flies away from the food."

She handed me a piece of cardboard and I spent the rest of the day fighting flies. For my trouble, she gave me a free sandwich and 25 *fils* coins. It was the first money I had ever earned. I was seven years old.

When I went home that afternoon, I begged my mother to accompany me to school the next day; but she was going to be busy with my two younger sisters. She also said she didn't want to be humiliated by the headmistress again.

My father was back from the mountains, but I never considered asking him for help. I knew the punishment I'd received from the headmistress would feel like an act of mercy compared to what my father would do to me when he learned that I had shown disrespect for girls. I couldn't ask my grandparents to intervene either because neither of them spoke a word of Arabic. My last option was my uncle, a young man who lived with my grandparents.

I begged him to visit the school on my behalf, but he apologized and said he had other commitments. I was desperate, so I threatened that if he didn't help me, I'd tell Grandpa about his nighttime rendezvous on the roof of the house with the Arab girl next door.

That did the trick. He put his hand over my mouth and whispered, "Hush, Hamko. You wouldn't really do that, would you? You know that he'd shoot me on the spot with his precious old rifle if he found out I was seeing an Arab girl." Though he didn't pretend to be happy about it, my uncle accompanied me to school the next morning.

After my expulsion from the school, my father decided to take me back to live with him and my mother in their rented room, along with my sisters, Shilan (who was two years younger than I was) and Dilan, who was only six months old. It was hard in the beginning and I often took the opportunity to escape back to my grandmother's house, but each time I did, my father soon appeared at the door. He didn't dare say anything to me in the presence of my grandparents, but as soon as we were outside, he gave me a few slaps to the face and warned me not to run away again.

My father was an illiterate man who couldn't seem to hold a job with a steady salary. He took on many odd jobs to provide for the family. One evening, he arrived home carrying a big stack of raw tobacco on his back. He dropped it in the middle of the room and asked my mother and me to help clean and refine it so he would be able to sell it the next day. We worked late into the night, crushing and smoothing the tobacco, sneezing as tobacco dust filled the air.

Early the next day, my father and I left for the city center. He carried the refined tobacco on his back and I carried the scale.

We found an empty section of sidewalk, set our tobacco on the ground, and I shouted, "We have the best refined tobacco from the mountains of Kurdistan! Come over here, roll a cigarette for free, and find out for yourselves!"

My father told me to keep shouting, but to skip the word *Kurdistan* and say only that the tobacco was from the mountains, in case people might be irritated when they heard the word *Kurdistan* in the city. Soon we were doing a brisk business.

What my father hadn't told me was that it was illegal to sell tobacco on the street and our entire pile could have been confiscated if he hadn't paid a heavy bribe to the policemen who patrolled the area. Most of the policemen were heavy smokers, so he had to give each of them some tobacco to make sure they would leave us alone.

One day in the early morning, a patrol pickup pulled up to the curb. I heard the officer in the car order two nearby policemen to arrest us and throw us and our tobacco into the back of the truck. As the vehicle moved slowly toward the police station with us locked inside, my father showed a half-dinar note in the palm of his hand to the policemen sitting with us in the rear of the pickup. Like a hawk, one of them snatched the note from my father's hand. Then, as the pickup slowed to a stop at an intersection, my father grabbed the sack and told me to jump out of the truck.

We ran as fast as we could through the narrow alleys of the old part of Mosul. We knew the patrol pickup wouldn't be able to follow us there. The two policemen jumped out of the vehicle and ran after us. My father knew that with me by his side and the tobacco on his back he wouldn't be able to outrun them. We knocked desperately at the door of a rundown house. A middle-aged man wearing an Arab gown and turban answered the door.

My father breathlessly implored him, "Please, we must ask for sanctuary!"

My father knew the tradition: if you knocked on an Arab's door and asked for protection, it was his duty to provide it. The man looked at my terrified face and said, "Come in, my friends. You'll be safe here."

Inside the old house, we found only a single room with cracked walls. The man's wife and half dozen children were sleeping on the ground, all under one dusty, torn blanket.

As we sat down, we heard a heavy knocking and men shouting, "Police! Open the door!"

The Arab man told me to crawl under the blanket with his kids. He then picked up a rifle, stood in front of the closed door, and asked the policemen what they wanted.

"We're looking for two fugitives," one of the policeman called from outside. "We want to search your house."

"There's no one in this house except for me and my family," the man replied.

The policemen knocked again, this time more insistently. "We saw them run into this house. Now you'd better open the door and let us arrest them or you'll also find yourself in trouble with the authorities."

I was shaking under the blanket as I heard the man cock his gun and say firmly, "These men have asked for sanctuary in my house. I'm giving you fair warning. I am holding a rifle and I would advise you to move away from this door before I start shooting."

I heard mumbling from outside and then silence as the policemen walked away. I poked my head out from beneath the blanket and saw the Arab man smile.

"It's over," he said. "You can come out now." He walked over and patted his wife on the shoulder to wake her up. "Woman, do you need an earthquake to wake up? We have guests for breakfast. See what you can do."

My father tried to refuse, but the man insisted that we stay until dark because he thought the police might have placed the house under surveillance. That Arab family was offering to feed us three meals, even though I could tell by looking around the room that they were living in utter poverty themselves. My father offered the Arab some money, but he refused. Then we gave him some tobacco, which he only accepted after a great deal of persuasion.

He never asked our names, where we were from, or why the police were after us. According to Arabic tradition, the person offering sanctuary has no right to ask the name of the person he has sheltered until three days have passed. But it wasn't hard to see that we were poor Kurdish tobacco peddlers, simply struggling to survive in a strange city.

One day I came back from school to find my family frantically running around the house, packing our possessions. I asked my mother what was going on. In an excited voice, she told me to hurry and pack my stuff because the government and the Kurds had signed a peace agreement. We were finally going back to our homeland!

Sitting on a heap of household belongings on the rear of a truck, I returned to my roots, to my motherland—Kurdistan. It was a place I had never seen but had learned to love through my grandparents' bedtime stories. As the vehicle approached the town, I saw a breathtaking scene in the distance. It was the first time I had ever seen a mountain. Somehow something stirred inside of me, yet I felt like I belonged there. It was as if I was discovering an essential part of myself that I had never known existed.

As we settled in one of the poorest neighborhoods of the town, I was eager to mingle with the other boys. It felt strange when, on my first day, some blond boys began staring me down. Then they attacked me, calling me "the Arab boy from the south, the son of a tattooed woman."

I cried out in Kurdish as I received their kicks, "My mother is not tattooed, and I am Kurd too."

I was frustrated with my inability to express my pride to those boys. I was proud to be a Kurd and proud of the beautiful land that surrounded me, but the rejection I received stung me. It took some time before those boys finally realized I really was a fellow Kurd, but when they did, they brought me into their gang—especially once I became friends with Rasho, the strongest and naughtiest boy in the neighborhood.

Every afternoon, we enjoyed the carefree feeling of just being out of the house. We gathered in the alley to hang around and play games with other kids in the neighborhood— girls and boys in separate groups, each with different games. Some of the boys' favorite games were *Chingany* (hide and seek) and *Tablany* (marbles) while the little girls loved to play *Pinjokany* (the five stones) and *Chollany* (hopscotch).

One day while the two groups were playing close to each other, all the boys suddenly panicked and ran toward the rocks on a nearby hilltop. I was left alone, but there was no time to ask questions. I ran as fast as I could to catch up with the boys. When I finally did, I found them hiding among the rocks with frightened looks on their faces. Breathlessly, I asked what was going on. They asked me if I had seen the man in the black Kurdish suit and white turban approach the alley carrying an orange suitcase. When I nodded, they told me that the man was the *sunatkar*, the man who performed children's circumcisions.

When they saw the blank look on my face, they explained what they were talking about. A chill ran through my body and I immediately threw myself behind the nearest rock. What I didn't understand that day was why the nearby girls also screamed and ran at the sight of the man.

We stayed on the hillside until dusk, when I finally felt it was safe enough to hurry home. Once there, I asked my mother fearfully if I would have to be circumcised.

She replied with a smile, "Hamko, you had a circumcision a long time ago—when you were only six months old."

Next time the town's child butcher was in the neighborhood, not only did I not run, but I was also filled with enough curiosity to follow him until he finally went into Sadow's house—one of the boys I really disliked. I was ecstatic. I was going to have the distinct pleasure of seeing Sadow's terrified face and hearing him scream in pain.

The house was full of relatives and neighbors celebrating the event and everyone was smiling—except for Sadow, who was sitting on a chair ashen-faced as he watched the *sunatkar* sharpen his blade. A moment later, Sadow screamed and tried to escape, but he was held in place by the firm grip of his father and an uncle. All the people then encircled Sadow, making it impossible for me to see what was happening. I had to kneel down and look between people's legs just to get a glimpse.

Sadow suddenly let out a huge scream of pain, combined with dire curses to the *sunatkar,* which were drowned out by the laughter of the observers as they assured Sadow that the ordeal was over. It was then that the celebration began in earnest as the women in the house started handing out baklava and *shorbat* to the guests.

Most boys in Kurdistan are circumcised between infancy and the age of ten. The family selects a neighbor to comfort the boy during his circumcision with the hope that the two will form a lifelong friendship. People from the Yazidy religion have a similar custom, selecting a Muslim man as a *krif* (friend) for the boy to be circumcised while seated on the man's lap, thus forming a blood brotherhood and kinship between the two families.

In early April, we kids had a habit of stealing green almonds from the farms in the foothills of the mountain. One day, two other boys and I were in a tree, giggling happily while we picked almonds and stuffed them into our shirts. We were too busy to notice that the owner had sneaked up and was standing at the base of the tree. We panicked as we looked down and saw him glaring up at us. We jumped down and ran in different directions, but I was the unlucky one. The owner decided to run after me.

As I ran, almonds tumbled out of my shirt. The farmer caught me as I tried to jump over a hedge. I was expecting the usual scolding and some strong slaps to the face, after which he would let me go, but to my surprise, he didn't slap me or say a word. He dragged me back to the tree where I had been stealing almonds. Then he took off his long cummerbund and tied me to the tree.

As he wound the cummerbund around and around my waist, he told me he was going to leave me there overnight as bait for a pack of the hungry wolves that had been coming down the mountain and creating havoc. I began to cry and begged him let me go, promising I'd never set foot on his farm again, but he didn't seem to hear my anguished pleas. He just walked a few meters away and resumed the plowing he'd been doing when the episode started.

After some time, I finally stopped my useless screaming. I felt some hope when he stopped working and approached me, but he just sat down, opened a basket, and unfolded a piece of cloth containing his lunch—bread and tomatoes. When he was done eating, he rolled a cigarette from his tobacco pouch and smoked it leisurely, looking my way occasionally. Whenever he looked, I did my best to muster a pathetic and guilty look so he would take pity on me.

Finally, he stood up, walked over to where I was tied, and asked, "Boy, will you ever come to this farm again?"

My voice quivering, I said, "Just let me go this time, please! I never stole anything in my life, and it was Rasho, the son of Halima, who talked me into doing this. I promise I'll never steal anything again!"

After the farmer untied me, I sped away, not daring to look back, and I didn't stop running until I was safe in my own house.

Our next-door neighbors had a cute twelve-year-old daughter named Miriam. I liked her very much, though she was a couple of years older than I was. After consulting Rasho about what to do, he told me to give her a wink. If she smiled or returned the wink, it would mean she was interested.

With Rasho's expert guidance, I learned the art of winking. I then spent the next day sitting near Miriam's house, waiting for her to emerge with her oilcan to fetch the family's drinking water from a nearby spring down the hill. When she finally came out, I stood up, took a deep breath, and gave her the most intense wink I could muster. To my amazement, she winked back and smiled sweetly. That encouraged me to follow her all the way down the hill, though I walked behind her, not daring to speak to her in public.

The spring was off-limits to males and fetching water was strictly a female duty. I waited in a place where I could see a crowd of women with metal cans jockeying for position to get at the small stream of water emerging from a cave. Miriam didn't join the fray but chose to wait patiently at the edge of the crowd. Throwing caution to the wind, I decided to break the taboo and go to the spring. I walked up to Miriam and offered to help fill her can. She nodded and handed the can to me.

As I approached the stream, the women turned on me and began to hit me with their empty cans, shouting, "You shameless boy, get out! You shouldn't be here!"

I shouted that my mother was sick and that I had no sisters, and to my surprise the crowd parted and the women let me move directly to the source of the water. A few minutes later, I emerged with a full can—and with my clothes soaked with water.

I handed the can to Miriam, who smiled when she saw my wet clothes. She expertly hefted the can onto her shoulder and turned to go back home with one hand on the top of the can and the other braced on her waist. As we walked, I wrestled with the urge to carry the can for her, but I resisted because it would have been embarrassing if any of the other boys had seen me on the road carrying a girl's water can. In our neighborhood, that would have been a serious act of shame and could have made me a target of ridicule.

Miriam was also nervous and asked me to go away before we were seen by a member of her family—that would mean trouble. When I told her I wanted to talk to her, she agreed to meet me at 3:00 behind her house, when the alleys of the town were nearly empty. Most people took naps at that time because of the heat. As she struggled under her heavy weight on her shoulder, I drew close and kissed her on her cheek. It was the first time I had ever kissed a girl. I was ten.

Then I ran to Rasho to tell him the news. His eyebrows rose when he heard I had not only had my wink returned, but I had also kissed Miriam and set up date with her that afternoon.

My mother was surprised when I told her I needed to take a bath, since it wasn't Thursday, our family's usual day for bathing. She also knew how much I hated taking baths. Normally she had to chase me through the neighborhood every Thursday and force me to take a bath. This time I sang as I bathed and when I came out, I ordered my little sister to clean my shoes. They had gotten muddy at the spring.

I set off toward the alley behind Miriam's house, whistling happily. But as I turned the corner of the house, I was shocked to see Miriam's big brother, Hasso, holding a thick stick in his hand. He gnashed his teeth at me like a mad bull and shouted, "You skinny insect! How dare you wink at my little sister? I'm going to teach you a lesson!"

He lunged at me with the stick over his head. In self-defense, I picked up a stone and threw it, which struck Hasso on the side of the head. The stick immediately fell from his hand as he reached up to feel the blood streaming down his face and onto his white school shirt. As he screamed in pain, I turned and ran to the top of the hill, where I stayed hidden among the rocks the rest of the afternoon. I knew Rasho had betrayed me and told Hasso the whole story.

As I neared my home that night, I saw my mother on the porch, taking off her plastic slippers and running toward me, barefoot. I didn't wait to find out what it was all about. I just turned and sprinted back toward the rocks.

When my mother realized she wasn't going to catch me, she threw both her slippers at me, which I successfully dodged.

She stopped running and shouted breathlessly, "Fine! You can run, but I'll get my hands on you sooner or later! I almost got beaten up by three women in the alley because of you!"

It turned out it was Miriam's mother and two of her aunts who had almost beaten my mother for the things I had done with Miriam. My mother was lucky to have escaped with only a severe tongue-lashing for raising such an ill-mannered son. I later learned that poor Miriam had also received a beating from her brother for damaging her family's reputation.

As my mother turned to go back home, I poked my head out from behind the rocks and shouted back, promising never to mess with Miriam's family again. I also begged her not to tell my father about it.

I was thrilled when my grandparents finally came to live with us in Duhok. I kept urging my grandfather to take me to visit Atrush because he was constantly mentioning his childhood village in his stories. His descriptions were so vivid that I could picture the mud brick and stone houses built on top of each other, the goats grazing on the mountainside among the alpine trees, and the ice-cold water of the natural springs that poured into a small river and then tumbled down the Belkeb Gorge. Each time I asked, my grandfather changed the subject or made an excuse, until one Friday morning he told me to dress up because my wish was about to be fulfilled. We were going to Atrush!

After a one-hour drive, we arrived at a military checkpoint, where they asked us in Arabic for our identification cards and then asked what we were doing in the area. Before I had a chance to display my Arabic language skills, my grandfather motioned for me to be silent. Our driver told the guards my grandfather wanted to buy some sheep in the nearby village.

As the car came over the last rise, a picturesque village appeared, perched on the jagged mountainside that gently melted into a vast valley. I felt strange when I saw two women in Arabic gowns walking behind a cow on the road.

My grandfather's eyes glistened with tears as he pointed toward a two-story stone house. Then he said in a trembling voice, "Hamko, that's the house I helped my father build when I was your age."

I was excited to finally see the place where my father and grandpa had been born and raised. I asked if we could take a look at the house, but my grandfather sighed and told me we couldn't get out of the car and walk around in the village because the government had banished all the native people and replaced them with Arab tribes from the south. It was at that moment I finally realized the true reason why our family had moved to Mosul.

As we drove further, my grandfather showed me a beautiful multicolored orchard nestled among the hills. The apple and apricot trees were laden with fruit. My grandfather asked the driver to pull over. When the car came to a stop, he got out— and I followed him. He took his small tobacco bag from his cloth belt and began to roll a cigarette.

After taking a big drag, he put his hand on my shoulder and pointed toward the orchard. "I planted all these trees with my own hands," he said sadly. "Now the only thing I can do is look at them from a distance."

As we got back into the car, a few Arab boys walked out of my grandpa's orchard carrying small baskets of fresh fruit.

They approached our vehicle and through the half-open window, they offered to sell us the fruit. Grandfather watched intently, devouring the basket before him with his eyes, then reached hesitantly for his wallet. *Would he buy fruit from his orchard?* He changed his mind, slowly withdrew his hand from his pocket and ordered the driver to start the car.

As we pulled away, I poked my head out of the window and shouted at the boys, "You don't belong here! This is our land and our mountains. Go back to your desert. You, sons of tattooed women!"

One afternoon while I was at the rocks, Rasho came running up to me and breathlessly said, "An Egyptian circus has camped nearby! There's belly dancing and you can see the exposed breasts and thighs of the woman!"

I didn't need to hear any more. We flew to the camp as fast as our legs would carry us. Luckily, it was the *Eid Alatha* feast, so we had received some money from our relatives. We bought two tickets and went in to see the show.

The hall was packed with men and boys gazing at the exposed curves of the belly dancer. It was a sight they never would have seen in our town. I enjoyed the view of the rounded thighs and swung my body happily to the rhythms of the exotic Egyptian music. At the same time I constantly looked to my left and right in the fear that I would be seen by a neighbor who would then report back to my father.

Since I spoke Arabic, I was proud to be able to talk to the dancer after the show. I also enjoyed the jealous looks I received from the other boys. The dancer thought I was a cute boy and granted me free entry to the upcoming shows—and I made sure not to miss a single one.

During the shows, I saw Mr. Issa, the butcher, who owned a shop near the circus. He took every opportunity to leave his shop in the hands of his young assistant so he could spend hours inside the circus tent gambling and watching the belly dancing show.

One night, I saw a big crowd in the neighborhood, with Mr. Issa in the middle. He was shouting, "This immoral circus is against our traditions. We must kick them out!"

At that point, I knew Mr. Issa must have lost a lot of money gambling at the circus. The mosque mullah supported Issa's protests and shouted, "Something should be done! The circus is against our religious principles!"

The crowd soon came to a decision. They would attack the circus and raze it to the ground. They also decided that the boys in the neighborhood would carry out the attack because the Iraqi authorities could jail the adult men for such acts, but the boys would be granted more leniency.

The men called for everyone to join in their holy mission, not knowing that most of us boys and Mr. Issa, had been at the circus that very afternoon, indulging in sexual fantasies as we watched the exposed body of the Egyptian belly dancer. I decided to participate—but only in the hope that I would be able to save my new friend, the belly dancer.

About fifty of us boys crept through the darkness then began throwing stones at the circus wall. After we destroyed the wooden gate, we broke into the circus grounds. All the circus staff members ran out in panic, leaving us free to begin the destruction and looting. I looked for the belly dancer, but I couldn't find her. I could only hope she had slipped out the back door.

While the boys were busy gathering their war booty, I heard sirens and then saw policemen rushing into the compound. I ran as fast as I could, but a policeman chased me down, caught me by the neck, and rushed me into a police van. They also caught several other boys before taking us to the police station.

A while later, I was called into the interrogation room. There, I saw two policemen, one of them was holding a thick black cable in his hand. After receiving several painful lashes to my body, I broke down and gave them the names of Mr. Issa and the mullah as the men who had perpetrated the attack.

As the summer holiday came, I finally got my father's approval to spend a few days at my aunt's house in a nearby village. My aunt's family had a donkey that seemed to be bothered by my presence. I tried to ride him the first afternoon, but he resisted. To irritate him, I pulled his long ears, and when he tried to walk away, I grabbed his tail and dug my heels into the ground, using my body weight to prevent him from moving.

I was enjoying the escapade until suddenly I received a strong kick to my face that sent me sprawling to the ground. As I tried to stand up, my head was spinning and I saw little stars twinkling before my eyes. Blood was running from my nose and my mouth was bleeding. I was lucky I walked away from that experience with my teeth still intact.

When my aunt rushed out to see what had happened, I told her that her donkey had gotten mad for no obvious reason and had attacked me as I was coming out of the front door.

Grinding her teeth, my aunt said, "You poor boy! I'll teach that donkey a lesson so he'll behave better in the presence of visitors. He'll be grounded for a week—no playing in the meadows in the afternoon. I'll also deprive him of his favorite meal—salty watermelon slices."

I couldn't tell if my aunt really meant what she was saying or if she was just saying that to make me feel better.

After she helped clean my face and put a piece of cotton in my nostril to stop the bleeding, my aunt told me she was going upstairs to make tomato paste from the dried tomatoes on the rooftop. I went inside, my mind consumed with how I could gain my own revenge on that donkey. The idea of putting mouse poison in his watermelon treats was very tempting.

Suddenly, I heard the roar of two Iraqi aircraft overhead and shortly after that, a huge explosion. It was so close that I was thrown against a wall. After I managed to get up, I remembered my poor aunt and ran to the rooftop, where I found my aunt lying in shock on a huge plate of tomatoes.

As I helped her to her feet, I asked if she was alright. She looked down at her dress and said, "I don't know. I'm soaked with blood. Go and get some help—quickly!"

I tried to hide my smile as I said, "Aunt, I think you'll be alright. It looks like you fell on the plate and you're covered all over with fresh tomato paste—not blood."

One evening, my father came back from his job looking worried, so I knew something had happened. He told me my uncle, who was a Peshmarga fighting against the Iraqi army in the mountains, had been wounded. He was being attended to in a remote village and was in urgent need of anti-inflammatory medicine.

My father had asked one of his friends who worked in the hospital to smuggle out some of the medicine, but he didn't know how to get it to my uncle. It would mean passing through a number of Iraqi secret police checkpoints and avoiding Iraqi army bunkers and then walking through no-man's land to reach the liberated area controlled by the Peshmargas. If captured by the Iraqi army or Kurdish collaborators, it would lead to either instant execution or death by torture.

As my father pondered who could be entrusted with such a dangerous mission, I said, "Father, I can do it."

My mother was horrified and said, "No! Son, you're too young for such a mission."

My father sighed, thought for a moment, then turned to my mother and said, "I think he can do it. He's so young they wouldn't suspect him." Then he looked at me and asked, "Son, are you sure you want to do this?"

"Yes, Father," I replied, proud that he would even think of entrusting me with such a monumental task.

That was the moment I left my boyhood behind me. I was thirteen.

The next day, with vials of medicine stuffed into my socks, my father and I drove through various checkpoints. Then he gave me directions and dropped me off at the end of an asphalt road at the foothills and I began to walk.

My excitement of seeing the Peshmargas, the men in red turbans, for the first time overruled my fear. The road was empty and silence prevailed, except the casual singing of birds. As I walked, I thought of my heroic mission. I would be saving the life of a Peshmarga who had been wounded in the fight against the Iraqi army. It would be a story I could repeat hundreds of times to girls to make them fall for me.

Suddenly, I remembered one of my grandfather's favorite stories about being attacked by a huge bear in the mountains. He had escaped death only by wounding the bear with his Kurdish dagger.

As I pondered my grandfather's story, I was startled by the voice of a man shouting at me from a nearby vineyard. "Hey, strange boy! What are you doing here in the middle of nowhere?"

I shouted back, "I'm going to Chamanki to visit my relatives."

Smiling, he waved his hand toward the mountain and shouted, "Only a half hour more and you'll be there."

I waved goodbye and continued my walk, until I saw on a hilltop the figure of man dressed in a red turban and holding a rifle. I started climbing the hill toward the man and when he saw me, he started down to meet me.

When we drew close, he held out his hand and as I shook it, he said, "Hey, city boy, what brought you here? Don't you have classes to attend?"

I said proudly, "I'm Silo Swary's nephew and I've brought him some medicine."

"Ah, Silo Swary! Poor guy" the Peshmarga replied. "There was a wedding in the village and Silo was watching the dance circle from a rooftop. As they brought the bride and the bridegroom into the circle, one of the boys in the wedding party held up a gun and fired into the air. The bullet hit your uncle, causing him to fall off the roof and right into the middle of the dance circle."

The man laughed briefly before continuing his explanation. "As you know, a Kurdish wedding generally goes on for three days, with dancing and lots of food, but when your uncle got shot, they called off the rest of the celebration. Apparently, the bride thought it was a bad omen, since most of the time bullets fall like rain and no one gets hurt."

My dream of fame and glory fell like my uncle from the rooftop. I sighed, knowing I had risked my life to bring medicine to a Peshmarga fighter who had been wounded by a stray bullet at a wedding celebration instead of on a battlefield. It definitely wasn't a story that would gain me any advantage with the girls.

My school was close to the soccer field. One day, armed Ba'ath Party members came to the school and announced they were going to take us to watch a football match. We were happy—first because we all adored soccer and second because we were eager to skip some classes.

As we entered the field, there was no sign of any football match—only a sizable number of men in military uniforms. Strangely, five iron posts had been set into the ground at centerfield. Our faces fell. We were in for another boring Ba'ath ceremony. However, our expressions quickly turned from disappointment to horror when soldiers brought in five blindfolded young men and tied them to the posts.

Things got even more tense when one of the boys from my class pointed toward the field and shrieked, "Oh, God! That's my brother, Samir!"

We rushed to the horrified boy's side and helped him to a seat as his sobs sent a number of angry armed men in our direction. We all knew we were about to be forced to witness an unbelievably barbaric scene, but there was nothing we could do about it. Some boys from the younger classes took cover behind older students while others threw themselves behind the seats.

A few moments later, an ugly overweight man with a thick mustache and dressed in an olive uniform began speaking through a microphone down on the playing field. His voice echoed throughout the stadium as he proudly announced they were about to execute five cowards. He pointed at the blindfolded young men and derided them because they had "refused to fight in our holy war with Iran."

The overweight Ba'ath official gave a signal to the firing squad and chanted, "Long live our glorious leader, Saddam Hussein! Long live the Ba'ath Party! Death to all traitors!"

The men raised their automatic weapons and when given the command they shot their captives down. The sound of gunshots rocked the stadium as the bodies of the young men sank slowly down the posts until they were lying in pools of blood. Then, with great flourish, the ugly man took out his pistol, walked to each of the bleeding bodies, and pumped a final bullet into their heads. Finally, he looked up at his audience and demanded that we all stand and applaud the heroic deed they had accomplished.

After witnessing the execution of his brother, the poor boy from my class disappeared for several weeks. One day several of us decided to risk paying a visit to his family. When we arrived, an older woman opened the door and graciously invited us in for a cup of tea.

When I asked about her son, she sighed deeply and said, "After his brother's execution, Dildar left for the village."

Though she didn't come right out and say it, we understood that he had joined the Peshmargas in the mountains. There were tears in her eyes when she asked, "Did you witness the execution?"

When we all nodded, she burst into tears and screamed, "My only wish was to recover Samir's body so I could bury him and have a gravesite where I could kneel down and cry. I spent the past few weeks searching through the town's dumpsite in the hope that I might find my son's body among the garbage."

We knew the authorities had refused to give the boy's body to the family and had disposed of it in their own way. Even worse, they insisted that the boy's father pay for the bullets they had used to execute their son.

During my high school days, we boys used to hang around the school gate during breaks so we could impress girls passing on the street in the hope that we could hook up with them. I didn't know if it was my approach, the way I looked, or the way I dressed, but I had little success.

After complaining to one of my friends about it, he suggested I try wearing a red shirt. He told me that for whatever reason, a shiny red shirt seemed to be a girl magnet. With nothing to lose, I wore a red shirt the next day as I stood by the gate waiting for my next potential prey.

As two girls passed by, I said as convincingly as I could, "Wow! They say there's a shortage of sugar nowadays because of the war—but look at these two sweet pies!"

One of them turned and replied, "Well, the war has showed us many wonders—but I've never seen a talking tomato."

That was not the response I had expected, but I refused to give up. I continued trying to entice girls until a white jeep pulled up and two Iraqi secret policemen jumped out. They grabbed one of my arms, dragged me to the jeep, and shoved me inside. Because the town's main secret police compound was on a hilltop overlooking the school, my initial thought was that the police had seen me accosting the girls, but as the jeep took off, I found myself blindfolded and handcuffed.

After seeing what had happened to the five young men at the stadium, I was terrified and didn't dare open my mouth. A few minutes later, I heard a gate opening—and I knew they had taken me to the most frightening building in town. Common knowledge was that once they took you inside, you came out in only one of two ways—in a coffin or completely insane.

When the jeep came to a halt, I was abruptly dragged out and I fell to the ground. I was immediately kicked several times. Then they pulled me to my feet and led me down a flight of stairs. When they removed the blindfold and handcuffs, I found myself in a cell in the dimly lit basement.

I looked down and saw that my red shirt was torn in several places. My nose and mouth were bleeding, so I tore off part of my tattered shirt and put it my nostrils. I also dabbed at the blood on my face and neck. I was in great physical pain, but that paled in comparison to the panic I was feeling at the terrible fate that might be in store for me.

The air was filled with a disgusting odor of blood and human waste. Glancing around my cell, I saw many dates and names engraved on the walls, along with a number of bloody handprints. I threw myself into a corner of the empty cell and tried to collect myself, but I knew there was a real chance that my life would soon end.

I waited in anguish for several hours until the same two agents who had seized me shoved the door open. They yanked me to my feet, grabbed me by the hair, threw me against the wall, and once again applied the blindfold and handcuffs.

As they pushed me up another flight of stairs, I stumbled several times, and each time I fell, they kicked me before pulling me back up. As we reached the next floor, we walked a short distance. Then I was led into a room and roughly pushed down onto a chair. Only then did they remove my blindfold.

As I looked around, I saw a skinny dark man sitting behind a table amid a haze of smoke from a noxious-smelling cigar. He stared at me fiercely and growled, "Let's not waste any time. Either you cooperate with us and confess everything, or you die under torture."

Trembling with fear, I said in a quivering voice, "Alright, I'll confess everything, and I promise I'll never be involved with such acts in the future."

The man smiled as he sat back in his large chair and said, "Good! Now give me the names of all the comrades who were with you."

When I told him I was alone and that nobody else was involved, his face turned red as he stood and approached me. He then raised his huge hand and slapped me across the face so hard that I fell out of the chair.

As the two agents grabbed me and threw me back onto the chair, the skinny man shouted, "You'd better cooperate and give us names! Now, I'm going to ask you again. How many are in your underground cell and who is the leader?"

I was confused. I had no idea what the man was talking about. I said, "Sir, what is an underground cell? I don't know what you mean."

My remark further infuriated the skinny man. He grabbed me by the shoulders and pushed me against the wall, shouting, "Boy, don't try to get smart with me! Do you have any idea how many other pieces of scum like you have told me the same thing?"

My mind filled with panic and terror, I said, "I swear, sir. I don't know anything about what you're saying. I thought I am here because—"

Before I could finish my sentence, I felt another stinging slap to my face as the man roared, "You said you were going to cooperate and tell me the truth! When did you join the Communists and who talked you into joining them?"

Now completely panic-stricken, I sobbed, "Sir, I'm not the guy you're looking for. There must be some mistake. I don't know anything about Communism. Please, sir, let me go. You seem to be a nice man."

The man roared with laughter at my comment, then shouted, "Me, nice? Boy, I'm a son of whore! If I wasn't a son of whore, I never would have ended up as an officer in the Iraqi secret police." Then, to my relief, his tone seemed to soften slightly. "If you're not a Communist, why on earth were you standing at the school gate, right on the main street, wearing a red shirt?"

As he asked the question, my eyes fell on a small TV in the corner of the room. At that moment, the image of Turob, a famous Arab singer, dressed in her signature blonde wig and a long red dress appeared on the screen.

I pointed at the TV screen and said, "Sir, does that mean Turob is a Communist, too?"

Suddenly, I felt a tremendous blow to my head—and then everything went black. When I woke up, I found myself in a hospital with my father leaning over me and my mother in a chair at the edge of the bed, weeping.

Early one morning while I was walking to school through the narrow alleys of the old part of the city, my thoughts were consumed with creating a convincing excuse not to do an assignment. Suddenly, I heard a woman scream from one of the nearby houses. As I raised my head, I saw a girl of about seventeen in a *dishdasha* (sleeping gown) rush out of her house. Two middle-aged men with butcher knives in their hands followed her.

One of the men pulled her back by the hair and both of them stabbed her repeatedly in the chest and stomach. The girl waving her blood stained hands in the air pleaded with them, "Please doesn't do this to your daughter! Please don't kill me!"

As the girl dropped to the ground, I froze in my tracks. Then one of the men grabbed the lifeless body by the hair and dragged it back into the house. The second man placed a bloody handprint on the upper part of the metal house gate as a badge of honor before he also disappeared into the house.

My heart pounded wildly against my ribcage, and for a long moment I stood motionless, shaking from the horrific scene I had witnessed. Then more screaming came from inside the house, probably from the girl's mother and sisters when they realized what had happened.

The next-door neighbor came out of his house and asked me what had taken place. Before I could tell him the horrific details, I asked for a drink of water. Seeing that I was in shock, he invited me into his house. I downed the whole glass in one long gulp, then told him what I had seen.

When I finished, he shook his head and said, "So, he fulfilled his part of the agreement."

"What agreement?" I asked.

He told me the girl had been in love with a boy and they had been meeting regularly in secret. The boy had sent his mother to the girl's family to ask for her hand, but the girl's father rejected his proposal, saying that they had already planned to marry off their daughter to her first cousin.

A few weeks later, the family discovered the daughter was pregnant. A vendetta was sure to break out between the two families and many people would be killed. Some tribesmen and the village mullah tried to mediate a settlement, suggesting that the couple marry and the boy's family offer a sum of money and one of their daughters to compensate for the loss of honor, but the girl's family, especially her uncle and cousin, said it wasn't enough. Instead, they insisted that each family kill the disgraced member.

"Now it's the other family's turn to kill their son," the neighbor said. "This family has cleansed its honor—and has given the town gossips a great story to spread around."

Hearing the man talk made me think of Samurai fighters in Japanese films, but when Samurais believed they had lost their honor, they didn't kill other people. They simply fell to their knees and plunged their swords into their own bodies.

I couldn't go to school after that incident. I turned around and went back home.

Over the coming weeks, I was haunted by many questions. Could I have stopped it from happening? Why hadn't I tried to intervene? Even if I couldn't have stopped it, why didn't I at least shout out? Then I convinced myself that I could hardly intervene in something that even our mighty government turned a blind eye to. When it was an honor killing, the government ignored it if nobody filed a case against the killers. And even if someone did bring such a case against the men, the father and the uncle would typically escape with a mild sentence of six months in jail.

My friends noticed I was acting strangely. Every time they started talking about girls, I either changed the subject or asked to be excused. I lost my appetite for girls altogether and made a vow never to touch a girl before our wedding night. I refused to be the reason some poor girl lost her life—simply because of a stolen kiss at the front door.

A few weeks after the stabbing incident, my friends convinced me to crash a wedding party. Weddings were one of the rare opportunities to meet unfamiliar girls and to have some physical contact during mixed dances. Another good reason for going was free food. My friends were hoping for some hand-touching, but for me girls were out of the question. However, I did fancy some free grilled chicken breast and a plate of rice.

At a Kurdish wedding party, the groom sits encircled by male guests while the bride sits on the ground wearing a translucent veil surrounded by women guests. The bride should look somber and never smile during the celebration to show how sad she is to leave her parents.

Solo Kurdish flute music signals all the people to prepare for a group dance. Soon after that, the sound of the *dahul*, a Kurdish drum, joins the flute to announce the main celebration. Men in baggy trousers and patterned cummerbunds hold hands with women in dazzling multicolored gowns for a mixed dance circle. The bride and groom sit silently watching the dances for quite some time before they also join in and the moment they do, people shower their heads with candy and coins. The wedding couple soon finds it hard to continue dancing as children race to pick up the candy and coins that land between the feet of the bride and groom. Sometimes the bride's dress is even torn during the ensuing chaos.

Girls in the circle often hold hands with male relatives, brothers, or cousins, but it's unlikely that they will accept the hand of a stranger. Therefore, if you attempt to hold an unfamiliar girl's hand, she'll often either pull it away or leave the circle. Even if she decides to take a risk and hold your hand, a furious cousin or brother soon pounces on you like a tiger and punches you in the face.

While my friends joined in the various dances, I sat smoking a cigarette by the kitchen door, savoring the smell of the grilling meat. When lunch was served, my friends and I ate as much as our stomachs could hold.

After lunch, people formed the dance circle. My friends grabbed me by the shoulders and tried to drag me into the circle, but I broke free. I watched the crowd until I saw a gorgeous girl join the circle. She held hands with a boy on her right and a middle-aged woman on her left.

As I watched the girl's graceful dancing, a huge force inside pushed me toward the circle—until images of two men plunging butcher knives into a screaming young girl flashed through my mind. I turned to go back to my seat, but as I watched the girl's long hair swaying while she danced, I thought about having her hand in my mine and our arms slightly touching each other as our shoulders moved to the rhythm of the Kurdish flute and drum. It wouldn't matter then if they shot me in the middle of the dance and turned the wedding party into a funeral. I'd die happy. I made up my mind to take that girl's hand in the dance, even if it was the last thing I ever did.

I broke into the circle, took her soft hand in mine, and danced as if there was no tomorrow, arm-in-arm, hip-to-hip, shoulder-to-shoulder. The exotic music and the ecstasy of the dance made me think of going to the next level, which was three hand squeezes, which meant "I—like—you."

I gave her hand three squeezes, without daring to look at her as I waited for her reaction. If she left the circle, it would mean she wasn't interested. If she squeezed back, it would mean she was. But there was no reaction at all.

As the dancing continued, I tried for another hand squeeze, again not daring to look up. Then I heard the sound of a middle-aged female voice, saying, "Young man, please leave my hand alone. The girl you're interested in has already left the circle."

One hot summer day I was riding in a bus, listening to the vehicle's radio broadcast songs glorifying the war with Iran. The bus slowed down at a roadblock and I saw a few armed men standing close to an army vehicle parked on the side of the road.

Once we came to a stop, a man in a military uniform poked his head in and asked for our identification papers. After he glanced at my student ID card, he asked me to step down and wait by the military vehicle. As I stood waiting anxiously for an hour, I was joined by a few more young men.

Finally, the armed man walked over to the vehicle and announced proudly, "Gentlemen, you are going to have the great honor of replacing some soldiers on the war front in our fight against the Persian enemy."

They herded us into the vehicle and we took off. I assumed we were headed for a military base. As we drove down the bumpy road, I summoned all my courage and told the uniformed man, "Sir, I'm only a first-year high school student."

He glared at me, then said gruffly, "It's only June. You can man the battlefront for three months and then go back to your classes in early October."

When we arrived at the Ba'ath Party main headquarters, we were forced to sign papers, then locked in the basement. Later that evening, my father came to see me, bringing blankets and a few extra clothes. He then tried unsuccessfully to persuade the Ba'ath members that I was too young to fight at fifteen.

The next morning, armed men took me and the other forced volunteers to a military center for a couple of weeks of training. I was the youngest among the trainees—and the most rebellious.

We were exhausted after our first day and looked forward to getting some sleep. We knew we would be awakened at five the next morning. In our barracks was an overweight trainee who snored like an earthquake. He was keeping everyone else awake, so about fifteen of us picked up his bed and carried it—and the sleeping young man—out to the middle of the training grounds.

At five, we were blasted from our beds by the blaring sound of a trumpet. As we lined up in front of our drill sergeant, he stalked back and forth, eyeing us angrily and demanding, "Who did it?"

His demand was met by complete silence, which made him even more angry. He strode forward, put his face an inch away from mine, and shouted the question again at the top of his lungs. I couldn't help myself. I smiled at the thought of the young man waking up in the middle of the training grounds.

The dark-eyed sergeant yanked me out of the line, yelling, "So you think it's funny, soldier? Well, let's see if you can take a joke!"

He ordered that my head be shaved on the spot, in front of everyone, then dragged me to an iron flagpole in the middle of the training grounds, where he shouted, "This will be your home for the next twenty-four hours!"

I suddenly had a flashback to the farmer who had tied me to an almond tree when I was a young boy—but this time I responded very differently. I smiled at the ugly sergeant in defiance. I was no longer a crying kid.

After two weeks of training, the military decided I was ready to join the war. I knew how to fire a gun, though I was one of the worst shots in the camp. I had endured huge cursing by the drill sergeant as my bullets hit the red warning flags on top of the hill instead of the targets set forty meters below.

The wait was horrible before my sergeant finally took me to the commanding officer to suggest which war front I would join. During training, I had heard frightening stories about various battlefields and how the Iranians attacked in never-ending waves, screaming "*Allah U Akbar*!" as they charged through barbed wire and minefields toward martyrdom, since their religious leader, Al- Khumayni, had given them each a symbolic key to paradise.

As I stood waiting in the commanding officer's room, the sergeant submitted my file. The commander looked at me, then at my file, and told the sergeant in Arabic, "You've brought me a kid."

He then scribbled something in my file, handed it back to the sergeant, and we left the room. Outside, my sergeant smiled as he looked at the file, then told me, "You're one lucky guy." He paused for effect, then added, "You're not going to the Iranian front. You're going to fight the outlaws in the mountains", were referring to the Peshmargas, my countrymen, my brethren.

I nodded my head in silence, not knowing whether to cry or celebrate. I had avoided the deadly Iraqi-Iranian war front, but

I was being sent to fight against my high school heroes—the Peshmargas, who were fighting for the freedom of my own people.

The next day, I was loaded into an army vehicle to report to my assignment. I asked the driver where we were headed, and he told me we are going to Dinarta, located at the crest of Pires Mountain. When we arrived at the military base, I reported to an officer, who decided to deploy me to one of the army bunkers on top of Sari Aqre Mountain. I stayed overnight at the base, then was provided an escort to report to my bunker. After about three hours of hiking, we reached the highest army bunker, which overlooked the town of Aqre.

Most of the soldiers in the bunker were like me—young men who had been forced to volunteer. I was exhausted from the long hike and fell onto a cot after I checked in, but I was immediately given a kick and a nasty look from an officer who shouted, "What's going on here? They're turning my bunker into a kindergarten!"

He told me to get ready for my first sentry duty that night. He also said that the next morning I would be joining a team of soldiers accompanying a mule down to the main headquarters to bring back water and food supplies. I would go down to headquarters with that mule every week from then on.

I resisted the strong urge to sleep during my first sentry shift. It was quiet and dark in the guard post overlooking the valley below. My shift finally ended at two in the morning and I collapsed on my bed. I freaked out as I adjusted my bed. There was a dead scorpion crushed under my pillow. The soldier in the next bed told me to check my bed every night before going to sleep and to search my military boots in the mornings for scorpions. He told me they kill an average of three to five scorpions every day in the bunker.

I woke up at six the next morning and soon began walking behind the mule with another soldier. It would take at least five hours to make the round trip.

After an hour, the mule spooked for no obvious reason and the other soldier lost his grip on the mule's rope. The mule immediately bolted. We gave chase as it left the trail and took off across the rugged countryside. That mule was valuable army property, and losing it would be worse than losing a soldier!

After some time, the mule disappeared from sight. We searched for a long time until we finally spotted it. Splitting up, the other soldier and I surrounded it. Then I grabbed the rope and held it firm.

However, we were now lost at the bottom of a gorge and unable to see either our bunker or the headquarters. We began to hike up the hillside, unaware of where we were going, until we were startled to hear a voice shouting in Arabic for us to throw down our weapons. In a moment, we were surrounded by a group of men in long beards and red turbans, all with their rifles pointed directly at us.

We froze as the men moved forward and picked up the guns we had thrown to the ground. Then, in broken Arabic, an elderly man asked our names, ranks, and army unit. I again summoned all my courage and replied in clear Duhoki Kurdish that we weren't with an Iraqi army unit. We were high school students from Duhok who had been forced to volunteer.

Another man asked, "Which school do you attend?"

"Kawa high school," I replied proudly, since our school was famous for supporting the Peshmargas and had sent a number of young men to join the Kurdish liberation movement.

I told him that my uncle was Silo Swary a Peshmarga in Barwary area. At that, all the men laughed as one of them said, "You mean Silo Swary, the one who was wounded by a boy in the wedding party?"

After I admitted that Silo Swary was my uncle, the elderly man told me not to worry and that everything would be all right. He said that the Peshmargas usually took prisoners of war to caves in the mountains to be held until a peace agreement was reached, after which they were allowed to go back to their families.

Then the elderly man turned to the soldier with me and said, "I can see that you're Assyrian. Which village are you from?"

My companion replied, "I'm from Amidya, and we Assyrians are your brothers. We share the same land and our villages are a main source of support for the Kurdish revolution."

The elderly man thought a few moments, then said, "We will let you go back to your bunker."

He then signaled for the other men to give us back our weapons, telling us that if we lost them, we would be put into jail for at least two years by the Iraqi army. When they were about to leave, I said, "Sir, we still have one problem." As he looked at me, I added sheepishly, "We don't know the way to the headquarters."

The old man tried to hide a smile as he shouted to the others, "Khalo, Mehsu, Azoo, escort these young men close to their military base and then return to the caves."

After a half-hour walk, we were within sight of the headquarters. We shook hands with our escorts and thanked them for their help, then continued toward the headquarters, still in disbelief that the "enemy" had shown us the way.

On my next night shift as sentry, I enjoyed the view of the moonlight reflecting on the mountainside as I thought about my situation. As a city boy, my only worries had been to dress nicely, to look at girl's curves, to smoke in the school bathroom, and to play cards and dominoes in the tea shop in the afternoon. I never cooked or washed my own clothes and I never had to go to the fridge when I wanted a drink. One shout to my little sisters and all my wishes were fulfilled. I was the eldest brother and I had long ago learned the worth of authority and dominance, forcing my sisters to be weak, naïve, and obedient.

I thought about the previous summer when my thirteen-year-old sister, who was only one year younger than I was, had become engaged to one of our relatives. On the night before the wedding, we had a tradition that the groom's mother or another older woman and two of her daughters would spend the night in the bride's house, applying henna to her hands and then taking her to a beauty salon the next morning.

My father was out of town that night, so the groom's mother asked my permission to take my sister out of the house. I replied firmly, "We don't allow girls in our family to visit beauty shops."

They tried in vain to convince me, but I insisted that my sister be prepared for her wedding in our house. I was filled up with ecstasy to the tips of my fingers and toes at my new role, the man of the house.

As I sat on sentry duty, my thoughts then drifted back to all the fun I was missing with my friends because I was standing in the middle of nowhere, holding a rifle I was expected to use against my own people. The only fun I had was walking behind a stupid mule for hours.

In my anger and frustration, I cocked my rifle, aimed it at the sky, and pulled the trigger until the very last bullet had been expended. Since it was around midnight, everyone thought we were under attack. The officer in charge rushed toward me, demanding to know what was going on.

I replied that I had seen something moving among the rocks. He ordered all the other soldiers to man the trenches, but when we had all waited for a long time in complete and utter silence, the officer looked at me suspiciously and said he was going to report me to headquarters the next morning. I immediately raised my gun in the officer's direction and told him if he reported me I would shoot him dead and then run to the mountains. Holding his hands over his head, he backed away and left without another word.

The next afternoon, that same officer told me to pack my stuff. I was being transferred to headquarters. I was excited! That meant no more scorpions—and no more mules.

Back at the headquarters, I was assigned to an emergency squad, which meant two hours of duty at the main gate and two more hours at night. The rest of the day was free, giving me time for cooking—and playing cards.

One afternoon during Ramadan in mid-August, I was scheduled for an afternoon shift at the main gate. The weather was hot, so I reported for duty in my plastic slippers instead of my heavy army boots. I also forgot to wear my helmet. I sat in the shade, loosened my military belt, and pulled my shirttails out of my pants. Then I dozed off until I was awakened by the sound of jeeps roaring toward the gate.

To my horror, I saw that it was the general's convoy. It must have been an unscheduled visit because when the general was expected, the headquarters would line up six guards at the main gate who would greet the general with a smart military salute.

There was nothing I could do. I didn't have time to run to my commanding officer or to rearrange my uniform. The only thing I could do was grab my weapon, which was hanging on the wall nearby, and salute as the convoy sped through the gate. As I raised my leg as high as I could in my best military pose, one of my slippers flew off and sailed toward the general's jeep. I had a distinct feeling that I was going to be in gigantic trouble when my commander was informed of my horrible negligence.

In a panic, I ran to my room—leaving the gate unattended—then sprinted back to the gate in full uniform, where I stood pacing in despair as I waited for someone to come and order me to the commander's office. I didn't have long to wait.

Fearing the worst, I knocked, then pushed the commander's door open and announced my presence while saluting as smartly as I was able.

His face red with fury, the commander roared, "You are a disgrace to the Iraqi army! You made a joke of the entire headquarters today in front of the general. Why on earth would you report for duty at the main gate wearing plastic slippers?"

There was no excuse, so I just nodded my head, waiting for the hammer to fall. Barely able to contain himself, the commander shouted to another soldier in the room, "Get him out of my sight and let him rot in the detention cell!"

Sullenly, I followed the soldier to the detention cell, where he opened the door and shoved me inside. In the dim light, I thought I was alone at first. Then I realized that Nasso was there, too. We two were the most rebellious men in the unit, but we had never gotten along with each other. That made things even worse for me.

As we sat in silence, I expected Nasso to clash with me at any moment. There were no words spoken for many uncomfortable minutes.

Finally, Nasso asked in a matter-of-fact voice, "Well, boy, what brought you here?"

"My name is Hamko," I said firmly, "and I am not a boy."

Nasso burst into gales of laughter as I glumly began my story—and he especially enjoyed the part where my slipper flew toward the general's jeep. When I had finished, Nasso surprised me by standing, walking over to me, and shaking my hand. Then, in a hushed tone, he told me a secret.

He said he was going to escape the detention cell that very night, then take his gun and go into the hills to join the Peshmargas. He pointed out a small hole next to a lock at the upper part of the cell that led to the kitchen. Some of his friends had managed to dig that hole using forks and knives. Picking that lock would be Nasso's ticket to freedom.

Despite our personal differences, Nasso knew I hated being in the Iraqi army every bit as much as he did, so he asked if I'd like to escape with him. I readily agreed.

The mood lightened considerably as we swapped stories about our various misadventures in the army. We discovered that we shared a passion for Indian films and both loved going to the only movie theater in Duhok. We also shared having to indulge our passion in secret, because if our families had found that we had been to a movie, we would have been beaten with a wooden stick or plastic shoe.

Our parents believed that movies taught immorality and took our focus away from school, but that only increased our passion for the cinema and we took any opportunity we could find to make enough money to buy a ticket. If there was a new show and we didn't have money for a ticket, we'd stand at the theater door and beg older people to hold our hands while they went in, because the theater allowed grownups to take one child in with them.

However, we weren't alone in trying to coerce grownups to help us get into the theater. There were lots of other boys with the same idea. If we couldn't convince anyone to get us in free, we'd jump over a wall into the yard of the theater and spend the next hour hiding in the toilets until the halfway point in the movie when they'd open the hall doors to the toilets. Then we'd join the crowd as people reentered the theater and watch the second half of the movie.

At about 3:00 in the morning, Nasso inserted a small knife into the lock, and after a long and tedious struggle, he finally managed to unlock the door and waited for the guard to pose for his morning prayer. When the guard was preoccupied, Nasso signaled to me and we rushed out.

As Nasso headed for his gun, I hid under a military vehicle and waited for him so we could run to the mountains. A short time later, the place was buzzing with reports of two escaped prisoners. Several soldiers found me sound asleep under the vehicle and I was led back to the cell and locked in. They never found any trace of Nasso.

After several days in the detention cell, I was released and to my amazement, was reassigned to my normal duties. One night at 11:00, we were roused out of bed and told to line up. We all thought it was going to be another false alarm and that we'd soon be told to go back to bed, but our squad sergeant announced that a soldier had accidently shot himself during his guard shift in *Lahasa*, my former bunker at the top of Sari Aqre Mountain. Our mission would be to retrieve his body before dawn.

The sergeant ordered four soldiers, including me, to undertake the mission. We were to move out in ten minutes. He ordered one of the soldiers to get the mule ready, then briefed the rest of us on our mission. Since it was a secret, we couldn't talk, smoke, or use any kind of lights during our trek.

As we headed out, the sergeant took the lead. I was second in line. The other two soldiers followed, leading the mule. There was enough moonlight for us to follow the path up the mountainside, but it was a treacherous three-hour hike to the bunker.

When we arrived, we found the soldier's body wrapped in a military blanket. We tied the corpse on the mule's back and started back down the mountain, but as we walked, the moon disappeared and the night became completely dark. We carefully picked our way along the path until one of the mule's legs slipped on a piece of loose rock, causing him to lose his balance and fall.

Although we couldn't see anything, we could hear the mule—and the soldier's body—rolling down the slope. The mule was fairly easy to locate, but we all had to get down on our knees and crawl through the intense darkness while we felt around on the ground for the corpse. Finally, one of our team whispered that he had found the body. We all moved in the direction of his voice and with a great deal of work, we retied the body to the mule's back.

After two more grueling hours, the sun was just starting to rise as we neared the headquarters. It was only then that I could see the disfigured body of the dead soldier dangling across the mule's back. It was a sight I'll never forget.

My military assignment as a boy soldier was finally over at the end of September, giving me only one week to prepare for the upcoming school year. I was eager to be reunited with my family and friends.

My mother was happy about the new things she observed in me. I had previously slept till 1:00 in the afternoon when I had no classes. I now woke up early in the morning, sparing her the daily torture of waking me. There were even times when I was up before she was. I also made my own bed and took my plate back to the kitchen after breakfast. I no longer ordered my little sister to clean my shoes nor did I beat her just to show that I was the man of the house. She was surprised when I opened my military bag and gave her a colorful scarf I had bought in Akra on my way home.

One morning, I heard my father tell my mother, "I told you to let him stay in the mountains for a while so the army could change him into a human being!"

Back in school, my most hated class was English. The only way I could pass was to sit beside a clever student on exam days or write all the irregular verbs and grammar rules on the palms of my hands. What made it worse was that the new English teacher, Mr. Jassim, would come to class sleepy and half drunk, filling the classroom with the smell of alcohol and cigarette smoke. He swore at us in Arabic more than he taught us English. Sometimes he'd tell us to open our textbooks and read silently while he smoked, the haze of his cigarette choking us, though nobody dared to cough or say anything about it.

Occasionally he'd read something to us, but since he was from the southern part of the country, his accent was hard for us to understand. He couldn't pronounce "p", sound so he replaced it with "b". A typical sentence like "Can I park here?" would sound like "Can I bark here?"

Then something happened that sparked in me a passion for learning English that Mr. Jassim could never inspire. One day, as I was sitting in a teahouse, a blind man sat beside me. He looked like a typical Kurdish villager, his shirttails hanging out of his baggy trousers and a worn checkered turban loosely rolled around his shaven head. I thought he was a beggar, taking a tea break before going to the gate of a nearby mosque and rattling the coins in his bowl as men emerged from the building after Friday prayers.

From the stirring sound of the teaspoon in my cup, he knew someone was sitting close to him. Turning his head toward me and putting both hands on his wooden cane, he said, "Salam, brother."

I replied, "Salam, uncle," expecting his next sentence to be either "Can you pay for my tea?" or "Can you help me to get to the mosque across the street?"

Instead, he asked, "Do you go to school, young man?"

"Yes," I replied.

Then he asked, in perfect English, about my classes. I stopped sipping my tea and stared at the man in disbelief. My first thought was that he might be James Bond, on an undercover mission to Kurdistan. He smiled when I answered in Kurdish that I hated English and would have preferred hard labor in an Iraqi jail than taking an English exam.

I paused, and studied the man from the top of his head to his dirt-covered plastic shoes. Then I asked, "How is it that you speak such wonderful English?"

He introduced himself as Simko Harky and narrated his story.

"I was born blind in one of the remote border villages—with only a few mud brick houses and no school. The children used to make fun of me, so my parents forbade me to mingle with them.

"In the morning, I used to walk with my father to our vineyard and help him, but my favorite time was the afternoon, when I accompanied my mother and other women up the hill to milk the cattle. I also had a privilege that no other boys in the village had. Being blind, I could accompany the women to a special place by the riverside where they bathed, giggling and singing for hours. Their singing mingled with the gurgling waters of the river.

"After dinner, the villagers would gather in one of the houses. The women would go into a separate room to hand-knot rugs. Those rugs were valuable property and families would only sell them under extreme circumstances or offer them as part of a daughter's dowry when she got married. The knotting sessions were also a chance to exchange the latest gossip about the village chieftain and his four wives.

"While the women knotted, the men and children listened to folktales told by one of the elders. Sometimes the tales took several nights to finish. I listened attentively and memorized those stories. Later, I'd sit in my room and retell them to my pet goat.

"One summer, we packed the grapes on the back of our donkey and my father headed to Mosul to trade them for sugar, tea, and other things our family needed for the winter. A few days later, I became excited when I heard the braying of the donkey. I knew my father was back and I could hardly wait to taste the delicious halava candy he always brought home from his trips to Mosul.

"As he shouted to announce his arrival, I began feeling my way out to him. When I reached him, my hand touched some screaming hens on the donkey's back, their legs bound tightly together. That would be good news for our rooster, since a disease had killed all the hens in the village earlier that year, and our rooster was 'the last of the Mohicans.' Now he would have female company again.

"I then felt for my father's trousers, asking, 'Dad, where's the halva candy?'

"He said he was sorry, but he didn't have any for me. I was about to cry when I felt him place a big box into my outstretched hands.

"He said, 'But here's something you'll really like.'

"Then he took my fingers and helped me turn a small button on the box. Instantly, I heard a voice from the box, speaking in a strange language. My father told me it was a new miracle called a radio.

"When my mother heard the voice coming from the box, she shouted in panic, 'The devil's soul is trapped inside that thing! I should go to the sheikh and make an amulet, then slaughter a hen to protect the family from the evil spirit!'

"As for me, I wasn't worried about the evil spirit, since I couldn't see it anyway. I was in another world, turning the radio knob to the right and left and listening to music and the sound of people talking. From that day on, the radio became my twin brother, my companion, and it changed my life forever. After thirty years of listening to the BBC and VOA, I not only learned English, but I also developed a knowledge of medicine through the science programs that helped me keep track of recent advances in medicine and drugs.

"Since medical care was almost nonexistent in the remote villages where I lived, I became the area's doctor, prescribing medicine for villagers who couldn't afford to go to urban doctors. A pharmacist taught me how to inscribe the English letters with a needle."

When he finished his story, Simko took out a piece of cardboard and a needle and showed me how he prescribed drugs for his patients, who then had their prescriptions filled at drugstores in Mosul or Duhok.

Simko Harky's story struck me like a punch in the face. Here was a blind man who had never been to school, had never learned Braille, yet had learned everything he knew from listening to the radio. At the same time, I was a young man with hawk-like vision that I used mainly for looking at the curves of passing girls. I had never used my precious eyes to develop any real skills that would help me with my own future. Sighing deeply, I stood, insisted on paying for Simko Harky's tea, and gave him such a strong handshake that his cane almost fell from his hand.

I began my freshman year at Mosul University, joining the College of Arts to study English Language and Literature. I had never experienced free interaction with girls, except for my first two years in elementary school, and I had always thought of girls as exotic, magical creatures I was supposed to protect—and dominate.

On my first day at college, I entered the auditorium and sat in the back. While I was listening to the dean's welcome speech to the new students, I spotted a girl sitting in the farthest corner of the room. I found myself wishing the world would stop so I could look at her forever. I couldn't take my eyes off her for a second.

I felt an instant connection with her, as if I were looking at someone I'd known all my life. Her long black hair and enchanting big black eyes dazzled me. I tried to concentrate on what the dean was saying, but I failed miserably. Suddenly, she flipped her hair back and turned toward me. Her breathtaking smile penetrated the depths of my soul and shook my very existence. I felt as if an electric current were passing through my entire body. I was on the verge of crying because I somehow knew, deep down inside, that she was the one for me. Cupid had worked his magic on me and I was suddenly hopelessly, helplessly in love.

The next day, I was delighted to see that incredible young woman in the room as I walked into my first class. Her name was Pari (which means 'angel' in Kurdish). I was so enchanted that I couldn't concentrate on anything else.

As the days went by, if Pari wasn't around, I felt an intense emptiness, unlike anything I'd ever felt in my life before. All I could think of, day or night, was her. If I tried to read a book, I saw her image dancing in front of my eyes. If I closed my eyes in an effort to concentrate, I saw an even larger image of Pari in my mind.

I was miserable when I couldn't see her and ecstatic when I saw her in class. I wrote her name in my notebooks and on all my college benches. I blushed every time I took a peek at her and I felt as if some invisible force were drawing me toward her. The feeling was confusing and depressing at the same time because Pari obviously hadn't felt the same irresistible attraction toward me.

For the next few weeks, I struggled to get Pari to notice me, but nothing happened and I couldn't understand why I seemed to be invisible to her. I longed for her to look at me and really see me, but she only glanced at me occasionally, her amazing black eyes showing no hint of emotion.

To me, Pari's fleeting glances seemed to be saying, "I'm afraid you're longing for something you can never have."

She was the ideal girl as far as I was concerned—beautiful, sweet, chic, slim, tall, and attractive—every man's dream. On the other hand, I was a short, skinny mountain boy with a nose like a pickle—a complete loser compared to Pari. It was hopeless. Never in a million years would such a girl notice that I existed.

I couldn't bring myself to reveal my true feelings for her, but somehow it felt good just to love her the way I did. It was all new and exquisite, in a terrifying and excruciatingly painful way.

Though I told myself I was free to love anyone I chose, it was torture to love someone so deeply who never returned the slightest bit of attention. I also knew I couldn't force someone to fall in love with me—but I did have the option to hang in there and hope for a miracle. Maybe someday we'd end up together, although I couldn't imagine how that would happen. Even so, I kept hoping, but nothing happened.

As the days went by, I felt even more vulnerable, as if I were being slowly sucked into a never-ending hole. Things were made even worse when I found out two other classmates also had a crush on Pari. I shouldn't have been surprised, but I found myself jealous and even more depressed, even though Pari never talked to any of the boys in class on her own. She would only reply if someone asked her a question.

Then one day, it seemed as if the miracle I'd been waiting for had occurred. Pari and I both signed up for a field trip to the ancient monastery of *Mar Matti* on Maqlob Mountain. I was beside myself with joy! I was finally going to get my chance to impress the angel who had captured my heart.

My first move was to ditch my usual college uniform—the white shirt and grey pants—and look for more colorful clothes. I approached my roommate in the dorm, who was a snappy dresser, but he refused to help me.

I decided to go back to Duhok and talk to my high school friend, Sherwan, who had always had a passion for nice clothes. After I told him of my predicament, he suggested that if I wanted to stand out among all the other handsome boys in college, I should wear a *shal u shabk*, a native Kurdish folk outfit. He showed me a milk-colored outfit with a flowery black six-meter cloth that was to be used as a cummerbund.

After he had shown me how to wear it, I headed back to Mosul. Part one of my plan was in place.

The other thing I needed to impress Pari with was food. I went to see my aunt, who lived in Mosul and was well known for a delicious dish known as *dolma*. I told her my story, finishing by emphasizing that *dolma* was a crucial step in my plan to win the love of the beautiful Pari.

Although my aunt agreed to prepare the *dolma* for me, she insisted on two conditions. First, she didn't have lamb meat, which was an important ingredient, so I would have to get some for her. That was the easiest one for me to accept. The second condition was harder, but I had no choice. She wanted me to take her unruly ten-year-old daughter with me on the trip.

I didn't have enough money to buy the kilo of lamb my aunt needed for the recipe, so I went back to my dorm room and stole some lamb from my roommate's fridge. I figured it was the least he could do to help me, since he had refused to loan me an outfit. Then, before I headed back to my aunt's house, I took out a bottle of pomegranate ketchup and sprinkled red juice all over his freshly ironed clothes in the closet. I wouldn't see him till after the trip, since I'd be spending the night at my aunt's house, but he'd definitely get the message that I hadn't been happy with his attitude.

On the day of the trip, I woke up at six, slipped into my outfit, picked up the *dolma* (and my bratty young cousin), and headed for the college, where we were to catch a bus. When Pari arrived, accompanied by several other girls, she looked gorgeous in her green *hawrami*. I was thrilled that she had also chosen to wear a traditional Kurdish outfit. I took it as a good omen.

Along the way, we sang songs in all the various languages spoken in Iraq, since the students on the bus were a mixture of Arabs, Kurds, Assyrians, and Turkmens. Some students even began to dance in the aisles. During the excitement, I took the opportunity to stare at Pari, though I was careful to turn my gaze away before she caught me looking at her.

By the time we arrived at the monastery, it was time to eat lunch and as various foods were spread out for everyone to share, I grandly poured my aunt's *dolma* onto a big plate.

As everyone began to eat, one of the girls exclaimed, "Hey, who made this yummy *dolma*?"

My moment had finally arrived. It was my time to stand in the limelight, but before I could pretend to be humble and say, "Oh, thank you. It's just something I whipped up last night in the dorm," my nasty little cousin shouted, "My mommy made it!"

I sighed deeply, faked a smile, squeezed my cousin's arm fiercely, and said, "You mustn't talk while you're eating," but it was too late. My moment had come and gone.

In the afternoon, we formed a dance circle to the sound of Kurdish music. I almost melted as I watched Pari dancing gracefully in the circle.

When my cousin asked if she could join the dance, I growled, "You should dance with the devil."

Tears filled her eyes at my remark, so I stood, took her little hand in mine, and we joined the dance together.

Later, the boys played some volleyball while the girls cheered. For me, it was another chance to attract Pari's attention. As the ball came flying toward me, I attempted to show off, but I lost my balance and fell to the grass, cutting one of my palms on a piece of broken glass. Although I felt foolish at first, I was amazed when of all the girls, Pari rushed toward me, and quickly took my bleeding hand in hers.

She started to dress the wound with her lipstick-smeared handkerchief. Her red lipstick blended with my blood. The mere touch of her hand sent shivers through my body. At that moment, I was flying over the clouds and dancing on a rainbow. I never could have imagined having the day end with Pari holding my hand in hers. It was the first time we'd ever been so close. I looked up at the long dark lashes that beautifully framed her sparkling black eyes.

She asked me in a soft, angelic voice if I was hurt, but I just looked down at the cut in my palm and said, "It's nothing."

A moment later, Pari's roommate, Sazan, brought a small first-aid kit from the bus and handed it to Pari. She then started to bandage my hand and I found myself blushing and feeling a little awkward as all the other boys stared at the scene in disbelief. All the way home, I couldn't take my eyes off the bandage on my hand. To me, it was a token of her love and I wished I could keep it forever. I was the happiest man on Earth that day.

The next day, the university was closed for the New Year's holiday, so I went home to Duhok. It was torture to be away from Pari for even a few days. On the eve of the New Year, I sat in my room, my gaze moving back and forth from the bandage on my hand to the rain drizzling against the window.

I had always loved the rain as a child. I thought of it as romantic. At night, when I saw raindrops glittering in the headlights of passing cars, I thought they looked like groups of dancing fairies. I never owned an umbrella, since I enjoyed walking in the rain. I picked up a pencil with my bandaged hand, and I wrote the following verse:

Wondering in vain
Is this love
Or have I just lost my brain?
Moaning in pain
I thought the night's mystic rain
Would bring you to me again
Tonight, the raindrops tap on my roof
I gaze through the foggy window
To catch a glimpse of your shadow
The rain stops
The New Year's lights appear in the sky
Reflecting the empty street
Once again my hopes die.

After the holiday, I was eager to get back to college and my classes—and to speak to Pari. When I entered the classroom and said hello to her, she asked about my hand.

"It's better, thanks to you," I said with a smile, but I still could hardly bring myself to look her straight in the eyes for more than the briefest of moments. "You were a lifesaver."

She smiled without saying another word and then we rushed to our seats as the professor appeared at the door. As I struggled to pay attention to the boring lecture, I slowly immersed myself in a fantasy world in which I heard a voice echoing in my head, telling me I needed to invite Pari to join me for a cup of tea. When the lecture was over, I mustered up every bit of courage and invited her to the cafeteria. She paused for an agonizingly long moment, then accepted my invitation.

As the weeks passed, our friendship grew and we became great friends, sharing tea, jokes, and laughs together. We even started going to the library to study. I was so happy she had stepped into my life, and I cherished every moment I spent with her. I wouldn't have traded her friendship for anything in the world—but something inside me wanted so much more. I loved her with all my heart.

The more time I spent with her, the more I realized how unique she was. I discovered the charming beauty of her inner soul, which exceeded her physical beauty. Everything she did and said held great meaning for me. Just to see her walk into class became one of the most special moments in my life. To me, she was nothing short of an angel walking on earth.

The pain was nearly unbearable and I was an emotional wreck. Even though a friend eventually introduced me to my first glass of alcohol, it didn't numb my pain as I crawled into bed and sighed in the darkness. I knew deep in my heart that Pari only had friendly feelings toward me, and nothing more. I was desperate to do anything I could to get her to look at me differently.

I started to focus on my English skills and worked very hard. Together, Pari and I worked on some everyday English dialogues and acted them out in front of the class. One day, while we were working in class, Pari's notes fell from her bench. As I helped her to pick them up, I saw a picture of a shirtless Tom Cruise showing off his ripped abs in the volleyball scene from the movie *Top Gun*. I finally had discovered who my real enemy was!

I immediately signed up at a gym and began working out regularly—with a photo of Tom Cruise taped to my training mirror. One day, a friend of mine noticed the photo and remarked, "I never knew you liked that guy."

With my arms shaking under the heavy weight I was struggling to control, I growled through gritted teeth, "I hate him."

By the end of the semester, Pari and I were the top students in the class and I was in much better shape—physically, but not emotionally. I was still disappointed that nothing had yet changed between us.

It was awful to be so close to her without being able to tell her how I felt. I wanted to break free from my miserable state. I wished I had strong wings that would carry me far away, but I was too weak to leave my cozy nest. I wanted to end the agony of waiting, but the mere thought of hearing the word *no* sent chills up my spine.

I longed for a way to let Pari know how I felt without scaring her away and losing her forever. One day, as I hovered between the world of illusion and reality, I heard a war was looming and that, as of the following day, all universities would close until further notice. That was the deadline given to Iraq by the coalition forces before they began air strikes.

That afternoon, confusion reigned on campus as students scurried around carrying their luggage. Amid the chaos, I couldn't find Pari anywhere. Then, to my relief, I saw Sazan walking toward me. I asked about Pari, and Sazan told me she and Pari would be leaving the next day to go home to

Suleimania, a city close to the Iranian border. I asked her to tell Pari I wanted to say goodbye at 10:00 the next morning.

I couldn't sleep that night, knowing that the next morning would be my make-or-break moment. I had to tell her everything I'd been feeling, because God only knew when we'd see each other again. My mind raced as I tossed and turned, and questions haunted my dreams when I did manage to drift off to sleep briefly. What if Pari didn't come? If she did come, what would I tell her? If I confessed my love, how would she react? I finally gave up trying to sleep and decided to write Pari a letter, in case I couldn't get the words out that morning. I sat down and wrote this:

Dear Pari,

I REALLY would have preferred to say this in person, but I wrote this in case I had no other choice. I hope by the end of this letter I'll be able to bring a smile to your face.

I've been avoiding this conversation for months, since I was afraid it might ruin our wonderful friendship. I didn't expect to feel this way for so long, but the fact is, there hasn't been a day since we met that I haven't thought of you. I think you're amazing.

I used to think that true love wasn't possible at our young age—until I met you. You're the first girl I've ever truly been in love with, and it's been the best feeling in the world. I feel so comfortable when I'm with you, but at the same time, I'm very attracted to you. For me, all other girls ceased to exist on the day I first laid eyes on you. As I got to know you better, I was sure that I'd never love anyone as much as I love you.

I have no expectations of you. I just wanted you to know that I'll always be there for you, no matter what. I also know that you'll always remain in my life in some way. Your love has changed me more than anything else in this world—and I'm a better person now because of you.

Now, with the war coming, we're heading in very different directions, unaware of what the future will hold. It may be months, or even years, before we see each other again. But please remember that no matter what may happen down the road, no matter what may break our hearts or what terrible events may befall us, I'll always cherish the warmth and the attention you gave me through your friendship.

If we are fated not to see each other again, I wish nothing but all the happiness of the world for you, to find the man of your heart, get married, and have kids. Still, I hope in the midst of the noise of life I will stay somewhere in the back of your memory. One day, while drinking a cup of tea surrounded by your grandchildren, you will remember me with a smile on your face.

Yours,

Hamko

The next morning at 10:00, I sat on a bench, waiting under a pine tree. As time passed and Pari hadn't show up, I stood and to paced. Finally, my heart began to pound as I saw her hurrying toward me. Before I could even take a deep breath and speak, she told me she only had a few minutes. She had to catch a bus that was waiting outside the gates of the college.

I felt as if I'd been run over by a truck. I made a huge effort to control my shaking fingers as I handed her the letter and said in a trembling voice, "Here's something I wrote for you, in memory of our friendship."

She blushed as she reached out and took the letter from my trembling hand and said, "Thank you. I need to run. I guess it's time to go."

"Yes," I said halfheartedly.

As she turned and hurried away, I fought the urge to grab her and hold her close, but I could only stand by helplessly as I watched her disappear through the gate. Then I threw myself back down on the bench. A flock of birds that had lined up on the power line above my head took off in panic as sirens went off throughout the city, signaling that the first wave of air strikes was about to begin.

People instinctively ran to their homes, and cars screeched to a halt, causing accidents as their drivers abandoned them. I stood slowly, picked up my bag from beneath the bench, and started toward the bus station for the journey back to my city. As I walked, my mind was a tangle of thoughts and emotions. I would cry beneath a big rock on Gara Mountain when I got home. I would scream and curse the cruel universe and my cries would echo through the canyons. But the mountains would embrace me like they always had and would offer me comfort. I would take heart in the sound of the red-legged partridges that sang in the valley and I would find solace as I watched the blazing sunset from the mountain peak. There would be hope again someday. It would soothe my tormented soul

In February 1991, after the Gulf War ended, life was paralyzed in Duhok. Schools and government offices were closed. The city had been without electricity for several months, and food supplies vanished from shops and warehouses. Ba'ath officials had cut the monthly government-supported food rations. People lived on previously stored supplies, which were running out. They stayed home, waiting for things to get better.

My father was glued to his battery-operated radio, shifting between two radio stations: the Voice of America Arabic Service and the BBC Arabic Service. He was hoping to hear America's President Bush announce that Saddam Hussein had been taken down.

In the afternoon, people flooded the teahouses to kill time. I spent most of my days playing cards or dominoes, smoking and sipping tea with friends. One day I was playing dominoes in a riverside teahouse with friends when war propaganda songs blaring from huge loudspeakers in the street disturbed our chat about our latest romantic adventures.

Suddenly, I caught sight of two Iraqi Ba'ath members in olive-colored uniforms hastily descending the stairs of the teahouse, looking very nervous. Without warning, one of them gave our table a vicious kick, sending dominoes flying into the air.

Then they grabbed two of us by the shoulders and pushed us toward the street, growling, "Come with us, you sons of bitches. You sit here playing dominoes while our country is in great danger. Get outside and march in protest against the American enemy and its evil allies!"

We were thrown into the approaching protest with all the other people who had been forced to march against their will and were marching in complete silence, their heads down, their faces filled with fear and disgust. I walked beside an old Kurdish villager who was leaning on a wooden cane. He walked slowly and could barely see through the cracked lens of his old pair of glasses.

I held his hand and helped him to march, whispering, "Haji, what are you doing amid this anarchy?"

He said, "Isn't this the march for rice? They told me to walk to a building where they would distribute two kilos of rice for each person."

I said, "No, it's a protest against Bush and the Americans."

"You mean Bush sent us rice?" the old man said, raising his hands to the sky to thank God for such generosity.

I quickly said, "No, Haji, there will be no rice!"

Upon hearing my words, the old man lowered his arms and slowed his pace. He coughed and leaned his weight on my arm as I helped him sit on the curb, too weak to continue the march. Then I continued on, sandwiched by armed Ba'ath Party members who were busy making sure no one tried to sneak out of the march.

We walked toward the Ba'ath headquarters, where we heard the threatening voice of a high-ranking Iraqi official shout,

"Why are you marching in silence? Scream slogans against the Americans!"

Fearing physical assault and verbal humiliation by the men in olive, we decided to shout the words to a Kurdish folk song about an old Kurdish woman. The Ba'ath officials would hear us shouting, which would make them happy, but since they didn't speak Kurdish, they wouldn't understand what we were shouting. We divided into two groups and shouted the following chant at the tops of our voices:

Who died?
A Kurdish old woman.
What was her name?
Totti Khan.
Where did she die?
On the mountain heights.
What happened?
She was eaten by a hungry wolf.

Our Ba'ath escorts were excited by our shouting. They waved their hands and nodded their heads, encouraging us to continue, thinking we were chanting slogans against the Americans. After we arrived at the Ba'ath headquarters, we had to listen to the usual long, boring speech about the Western conspiracy against Iraq, the only country in the world that had defeated a coalition of thirty countries.

Upon returning home, we realized the purpose of the protest had been to force people into the streets so they couldn't watch television and hear President Bush's speech, calling upon the Iraqi people to overthrow Saddam.

The following afternoon, we saw two American planes flying over the city to drop leaflets. Some of the leaflets landed in the foothills of the White Mountains, near where we lived. As curious young men, my friends and I decided to fetch some of them. After hiking a few hundred meters uphill, we found papers scattered among the rocks. I picked one up and saw that it contained a message in Arabic signed by the allied forces, encouraging Iraqis to revolt against their government.

Gradually, Ba'ath Party members and secret police started to disappear from the streets. Word had spread that the governor and the highest Ba'ath officials in town had fled south to Mosul. Some Kurdish towns close to the Iranian border had revolted and an uprising in the north had begun. By evening, we heard scattered gunfire in parts of the city. We were certain it would be the last night of the regime. The next morning, the uprising started in our own city and the sun of freedom emerged for the first time in more than thirty-five years of oppression.

In the absence of government forces or agents, groups of armed young men began to appear in our neighborhood. I sneaked out and joined them, despite my father's 10:00 p.m. curfew. The young men told me that most of the government agents had taken shelter in a fortified secret police compound on a hilltop overlooking the city center. That compound would be the main target by Kurdish rising the next day, since it was a symbol of the tyranny that had caused many people to be tortured to death in Saddam's cells.

Though I had once been badly beaten in that building, that wasn't going to be my target. I had another place in mind. I tiptoed into my father's room, where he hid his automatic weapon. Then I placed the gun under my pillow and waited for morning to come.

At the end of the '80s, my father and I owned a photographic shop. After the war with Iran, Saddam Hussein had directed most of his army units toward the Kurdish territories in the north to destroy 4,500 villages in a military campaign called the *Anfal*. The city was choked with soldiers and military vehicles pulling cannons.

One morning, while I was serving customers, a man in an Iraqi military uniform appeared in the shop door. Seeing a telephone on the desk, he demanded that he be allowed to make a long-distance call to a city in the south. My father told him politely that we didn't offer telephone services, suggesting that the man go to the local post office to make his call.

The Iraqi started cursing the Kurds and the legendary Kurdish leader, Mustafa Barzani. My father, still calm, said, "We are only shopkeepers, trying to make a living. We don't get involved in politics, but Barzani's men are in the mountains. Why don't you go up there and fight them?"

When he heard that, the man grew furious and pushed my father against the wall, sending photo frames crashing off the shelves. My father began picking up the frames as he again asked the Iraqi to leave, but I lost control of myself. I grabbed a pair of scissors and tried to stab the Iraqi in the belly.

As my father rushed forward and wrenched the scissors from my hand, the Iraqi moved toward me threateningly. My father raised the scissors above his head and shouted, "You've already caused a lot of damage around here. Now get out!"

The Iraqi walked toward the door, he growled, "I'll make sure you never see another sunrise."

After the Iraqi had gone, my father looked at me and said, "Are you out of your mind, trying to stab a man in an Iraqi army uniform?" I tried to protest, but my father cut me off. "That's enough. Let's start cleaning up this mess."

Although he was angry and frustrated, the look in my father's eyes told me that he was proud of me. For the first time in my life, I had managed to earn my father's approval. When he went upstairs to develop some photos, I ran out of the shop and managed to get a glimpse of the Iraqi as he got into a military vehicle on the side of the road. I drew closer until I could see the logo and number of his unit.

Now after a few months, my moment of vengeance has finally arrived. Lying in bed, I knew that the next morning would be a big day. I would restore my family's honor and avenge my father's humiliation. At the first light of dawn, I took my father's gun and headed toward that Iraqi's unit headquarters. I wanted to get to him before anyone else could. But when I reached the fortress, the army had already surrendered without a fight. I saw many young Kurdish men in groups, waiting for the arrival of the Peshmargas. I also saw many Iraqi soldiers on their knees, now prisoners of war, and I searched among them for the one who had humiliated my father.

When I finally saw him, he was kneeling, his head down in terror and anticipation. He knew what the Iraqis had done to the Kurdish people and was expecting the worst. I had planned to kill him as soon as I caught sight of him. I walked toward him, determined to drag him behind the building and administer the fate he deserved.

Then, before I could say anything, he looked up and cried, "Young man, I beg you. I'm dying for a glass of water. Could you kindly fetch me some?"

Stunned by his impertinence, I growled, "Do you remember me?"

He looked at me, then shook his head.

"I'm the son of the man you humiliated in our photo shop a few months ago."

Upon hearing this, the color drained from his face. He grabbed my hand and tried to kiss it, begging, "Please don't kill me. I hadn't talked to my own family in months, and I'd only been married for two months when they sent me here. I just wanted to talk to my wife and my family, I swear!"

I looked down at the pitiful figure. He was a human being, just like me, and killing him wouldn't bring any honor to me or my family. If I treated him like the Iraqis had treated us, we would be no better than they were. I turned around, picked up the nearest cup, and filled it with water from a tap.

As he reached for the cup, the Iraqi said, "Oh, thank you, thank you."

I asked him to stand, but he looked hesitant. I said, "I'll help you get back to your family."

I led him to our house, where I found my father sitting on the sidewalk, playing backgammon with a neighbor in the warm spring sun and drinking black Kurdish tea. When he saw me, he asked, "Hamko, what are you doing with this Iraqi soldier? Let him go."

The soldier rushed to my father, kissed his hand and said, "Haji, I'm very sorry for that day in your shop."

My father looked surprised. I explained, "Father, this is the Iraqi Rambo who destroyed our shop."

My father smiled and said, "Oh, him." Then he added, "Hamko, tell your mother we're having a guest for lunch."

We went inside the house, where we let him take a shower and gave him some civilian clothes. After lunch, my father told him he'd arrange transport to his home in southern Iraq. That afternoon, I rode with the Iraqi in a taxi to the last Kurdish checkpoint, then bid him goodbye and good luck.

On the way back home, I saw hundreds of women and children in front of their houses, waving happily to armed young men as they rode in the backs of pickups, roaming the streets waving Kurdish flags and shooting into the air in celebration of a new era. We thought we were on the cusp of independence and that our dream of a free Kurdistan was finally looming on the horizon.

While we were still drunk with the ecstasy of potential freedom, President Bush allowed Saddam Hussein to massacre us and did not intervene. The Iraqi army may have been weak, but Saddam Hussein gathered his forces, crushed the Shiite uprising, and sent his troops toward the Kurdish region to recapture the territory. Panic broke out. We knew what it meant when the Iraqi army raided a Kurdish city. We would be savagely crushed.

Soon Iraqi tanks and helicopters converged on the area and bombed the cities. Some two million people packed their belongings and rushed to the borders as fast as they could.

They began the dangerous hike through the mountains to Iran and Turkey.

My family gathered to discuss the matter. Staying meant certain death. Our city was close to the Turkish border, so we decided to flee to the mountains of northern Kurdistan in Turkey.

Since our family only had one vehicle, priority was given to the women and children. My father assigned me the task of leading the family's seven goats to Turkey. I tried to protest, astonished that even though hundreds of thousands of women, children, and old people were fleeing the impending invasion of the Iraqi army as artillery shells fell on the suburbs of the city, he wanted me to accompany his precious goats to the border!

Although it made no sense, I finally accepted the mission, which meant I had to leave before anyone else in the family if I were going to reach the border safely. My mother, wiping her tears, handed me a bag filled with dry bread and almonds. Then I set off with the hope of reuniting with the family at the border in a few days.

As I left the city, I saw hundreds of families, carrying whatever they could on their backs, lining both sides of the road. Many were crying while others simply walked slowly, sadly facing the great unknown. A boy pushed a muddy wooden carriage filled with blankets and food supplies. Other boys led limping grandmothers. I heard huge explosions, but could not see where they hit.

A young man called out as he passed me, "Hey, goat man, what are you doing with these strays? Save your own skin! Can't you hear the explosions?"

People were startled by any strange sound and watched the sky in fear of helicopters. A few kilometers northeast of the city, two copters flew toward us. Panic broke out as the helicopters dropped a white powder over the city. Was it a chemical attack? People scattered in every direction, covering their faces with pieces of cloth.

With one hand holding a wet piece of cloth to my face, I hurried the goats up a hill, where I joined hundreds of other panic-stricken people, all waiting for the effects of the chemical poison to take hold. The helicopters faded into the distance and the powder settled to the ground—but nothing happened.

It was then that we realized the army was spreading white flour over the city to terrify people and make them abandon the area more quickly.

The further I walked, the more horrendous the scenes were. The number of refugees increased dramatically. Women, children, and old people collapsed due to the great distances they had traveled and the effects of fear. People sat beside the road trying to catch their breath while other members of their families shouted that there was no time for breaks and urged them to stand and keep walking.

The most amazing thing was some were still smiling and talking during the march, but the fear of the unknown and the look of defeat were clear on most faces. For me, the most pathetic were the children, stricken with cold, some wearing filthy clothes and half-torn shoes. Many others were walking with their bare feet pressed into the mud. Families threw away food or other supplies so they could carry their children who after trekking for several hours, became fatigued and sick. It was a common sight to see a woman with a child on her back and holding the hands of two more children.

At first, for some boys it seemed like a nice jaunt into nature. Some of them were playing and giggling. I heard a father harshly reproaching his ten-year-old boy after hearing him laughing.

The man cried loudly, "It is not time for laughing. Don't you realize what's happening? Death is waiting for us all."

After several more hours, I reached Bagera, a village north of Duhok. The sun was disappearing behind the mountain, so I decided to stay in the village and set out early in the morning. Exhausted, I fell to the ground in a grassy field as the goats grazed nearby in the gathering darkness.

Soon clouds gathered overhead, announcing a spring shower. The village was overflowing with people and hundreds of families had to spend the night outdoors in a heavy rain. A family nearby managed to start a fire and more than forty women and children struggled to get close enough to feel a touch of heat.

For some reason, just the sight of the fire made me feel better. It was a light in the midst of complete darkness. I couldn't even think of sleeping, because my clothes were soaked and I found myself shivering in a night wind. The ground was muddy and wet, so I stood watching the goats as they formed a tight circle against the rain and wind. I had seen people go by hundreds to the mosque to pray for rain during a drought, but that night I heard them praying for the rain to stop.

Beaten by the wind and the rain, I eventually could no longer stand. I sat on the muddy ground. At that moment, all I could think about was holding a cigarette in one hand and a glass of hot black tea in the other. While I was having that fantasy, I must have passed out.

I awoke to the sound of a crying baby. The first light of dawn was peeking over the horizon and the rain had stopped. I looked around and was terrified to see that the goats were gone. Shivering in the cold morning air, I began my search. After a few minutes, I managed to find five of the seven goats. The other two seemed to have escaped during the night.

As I rejoined the thousands of people on the road, I forgot all about the war, the army, the aircraft raids, and my miserable situation. All I thought about was how to tell my father I had lost two goats.

I walked another whole day and arrived in the village of Mangesh, again exhausted, but thankful there was no rain. I went to the village mosque, hoping to find a place to lie down, but the mosque was so packed that there wasn't room even for another man's foot inside.

I spoke briefly to the clergyman in charge of the mosque, who told me he was a man of God and had no intention of leaving the village. He planned to hide in the mosque until the Iraqi army left. I didn't want to discourage him by telling him that if the Iraqi army did come to his village, their very first shell would hit the minaret of his mosque. Then they would use the mosque as their headquarters, line villagers against the mosque's walls (himself included), and execute them.

As we talked, I came up with an idea that would let me get rid of the remaining goats. I told him I would give him the five goats so he could offer them to the Iraqi army when they arrived. Offering the soldiers goat meat might save his life. If the army failed to reach the village, I asked that he take care of the goats until I could return for them in a month or so. If I didn't return after that time, he could keep them. He liked the idea, and we made a deal.

A heavy burden had been removed from my shoulders. I was as free as a bird to fly in any direction. I could honestly tell my father I had left the goats in the hands of a clergyman who had vowed to take care of them until we returned.

Now the most important thing was to find a place for the night. I really needed some sleep. Looking around, the clergyman said, "You can see that if you threw straw into the sky, it wouldn't land on the ground," referring to the thousands of people gathered in the village.

He then told me of a place I could sleep, if I dared to spend the night there. He pointed to a small locked room on his left. It was a special bathroom where they washed the bodies of the dead before wrapping them in white shrouds for burial. Since I was about to collapse after two days of walking and little sleep, I told him I would not mind sharing a grave that night.

The next day I set off again. I passed groups of men digging simple holes just deep enough to contain the bodies of infants, children, and old people who hadn't survived the long, harsh journey. Other bodies were left unburied along the road with only small pieces of cloth covering their faces.

I passed a baby wrapped in a filthy hand-woven Kurdish blanket, left unattended beside a large rock. I could not tell if it was alive or dead. I paused for a moment, not daring to lift the blanket, but something inside pushed me to see if the baby was still alive. My heart pounded as I lifted the blanket. Then I jumped back in horror at the sight of the child's yellow, bloodless, milky-eyed corpse.

I continued my walk with the crowds along a potholed asphalt road that soon degenerated into a muddy footpath. The blossoms on the trees announced the coming of a new spring. The valley was alive with flowers of all colors. As I walked, I thought back to an earlier time.

In my country, spring brings us hope, the beauty of the land—and tragedy. People feel uncomfortable because it's the time of the year when trouble begins. With the melting snow and the blooming flowers come the Iraqi military campaigns. The green virgin meadows are raped by converging tanks and marching black boots. In the spring, the morning breeze can carry poison clouds of yellow smoke drifting across the mountains. Our springs often start out green and end up blood-red. Over the years, the villagers have undergone the same tragic events so often that these attacks have become part of their lifestyle.

The story generally goes like this:

A family in the village gets up early to the sound of roosters and the singing of birds. Goats and hens wander loose around the yard. The husband heads to the orchard to irrigate the apple and peach trees while his wife prepares to go up on a nearby hilltop to milk the sheep. Their ten-year-old son, wearing his trusty slingshot, gets ready to take the goats to the grazing area.

The mother shouts for her eight-year-old daughter to attend to her crying baby brother in his wooden cradle on the roof of the mud brick house. The little girl, still half asleep, dutifully begins rocking the cradle and singing a Kurdish lullaby.

Suddenly, the morning stillness is shattered by the sound of a huge explosion as a shell hits the roof of the house, sending debris in every direction. The lullaby stops. The mother runs toward the house, screaming hysterically. Halfway to the orchard, the father also turns and hurries back toward the house.

To their horror, they find that their daughter and six-month-old son have been killed by the blast. Grief-stricken, the parents run as fast as they can to a nearby mountain cave, carrying the bodies of their children in their arms. They know it won't be long before Iraqi tanks, backed by the Jash (pro-government Kurdish militia), will come to loot the village. They will torch the houses and fields and execute all males above the age of twelve. Then they will force the remaining women and young children into military trucks to be taken to the Arabian desert in the south, where they'll be executed and tossed into freshly dug mass graves.

In the cave, the villagers bury the girl and what is left of the baby. As they dig, they can smell the black smoke rising from their houses and orchards. The ten-year-old boy, his eyes full of tears, looks at the graves of his brother and sister, then down into the valley, where soldiers and Kurdish collaborators slaughter his goats with bayonets. Those soldiers will later have a feast to celebrate their triumph over the hapless villagers.

When the burial is finished, the father sits on a rock, numbly holding a cigarette between his trembling fingers as he listens to the houses crumble and gunfire echo through the valley. Then he stands and walks over to his weeping wife, who is on her knees between the two graves.

As he helps her to her feet, he says softly, "One day, all this will end."

As I continue walking, I find myself wondering. Running to the mountains was such a part of our village lifestyle that I wonder if the caves aren't our real homes. They protect us, embrace us, and give us solace. However, there have been times when even the caves offered scant protection against bombs loaded with mustard gas or nerve gas.

The mountains have always been there to share our good times and our tragedies. They have been our only true friends. When we are in agony, they hear our screams echo through their valleys, blending with the cries of the eagles. Then the mountains weep their white tears into streams that flow down their sides.

When the few good days come, we celebrate at the foothills of the mountains. The soft winds carry the melodies of our folk songs and ballads through the canyon all the way to the peaks. Our mountains have taught us many lessons over the centuries. They shook at times, but they never fell. They continue to stand proud and erect, resolutely facing whatever comes their way, without complaint.

When the soldiers come, the villagers hide in the caves for a few days and then re-emerge and return to their burned-out houses and scorched fields. Then the collective work begins as they pick up their shovels and axes and the sound of folk songs again rises as they plant new seeds amid the ashes.

Thinking of my home and the people I love, I walked all day along the mule and goat paths that led across the steep mountain slopes toward the opposite side of the valley. The last rays of the sun were rapidly disappearing behind the hills. I was exhausted, hungry, and wet.

I knew a long night awaited me, so I stopped near some oak and pine trees on the edge of a ridge. The early March air was crisp and cold, and a fierce wind howled overhead as I collected pine needles and oak leaves to keep myself warm. I stuffed my pants and shirt with the oak leaves for insulation. Then I lay on my back on a patch of level ground and covered myself with pine needles from my toes to my head, but that wasn't enough to keep me from shivering.

To distract myself, I looked up into the clear night sky at thousands of shimmering stars. There is nothing like stargazing in the mountains to make a person feel as if he is only a small part of an infinite universe. Then I saw Pari's face twinkling among the stars, looking down at me with her heavenly smile. I felt some warmth in my body as my heart began to tingle back to life, kindled by the fire of my flickering love. I called out her name, but she did not answer. I stretched my arms for her to come to me, but she did not move.

Then I passed out into a sound slumber and dreamed that Pari and I were at college again. We sat together on a bench and I confessed my love to her. She smiled as I took her sweet hands in mine. I ran my fingers gently through her hair. The moment our eyes met, I kissed her on her forehead. But as I felt the tip of her nose press against my neck, I woke up, feeling itchy all over my body. The pine needles had crept into my nose, ears, and hair.

In the intense darkness, I stood at the edge of the mountain ridge and screamed at the top of my lungs, "Where are you, my Pari?" Her name echoed through the vast valley.

It was so freezing cold that I couldn't bear the situation any longer. Occasionally, I sang a song and danced to keep myself warm. I ended up doing every dance I knew over the course of the long black night. As I jumped and whirled, the oak leaves came tumbling out of my clothes and fell to the ground. I kept a close eye on the horizon, desperately waiting for the first pale light of a new day to appear. The following morning, as the birds were beginning to greet the first light of dawn, I was up and walking again.

After hiking for some time, I finally arrived at the other side of the ridge, where I rested while I took out the last chunks of dry bread that were left in my hand-woven shoulder bag. In the far distance, a fine haze of white smoke hung over Barwary Valley. When I finished eating my meager breakfast, I started toward the last Kurdish village before the border.

Upon my arrival, I encountered a scene of complete chaos and utter devastation. The canyon was filled with hundreds of thousands of shadowy faces—refugees who had gathered there over the past few days in the hope of crossing to safety on the Turkish side of the border.

Children wore mismatched shoes or were barefoot. Old men and women sat in the freezing mud, shivering under filthy blankets. In the midst of the destruction, I searched for my own family.

A thorn had found its way into my foot through a hole in my torn shoe, making me limp painfully. As I was wondering if I might come across an abandoned pair of shoes, I saw a man in striped pajamas walking toward me. He had apparently still been in bed when the shelling began. He stopped and took off his shoes to wash his feet in preparation for his Muslim prayers. He turned to the south, his shoes close beside him, and began to pray in his bare feet.

I rushed up behind the man, snatched the shoes, and ran until I was able to hide myself amid the huge crowd of confused people milling around aimlessly. I kept running for a while, knowing that the man would soon finish his prayers and begin looking for the culprit who had stolen his shoes. Finally, satisfied that I was safe, I sat on a large rock to try on the shoes. I was happy they fit, though I couldn't feel totally at peace with the fact that I'd stolen them.

As I stood up, I heard the loud shouts of the man, cursing the thief who had stolen his shoes—and I couldn't blame him. After all, climbing a mountain cliff to reach the border in such freezing cold in only his pajamas and bare feet wouldn't be easy.

As I walked aimlessly, I saw Hizo, a mentally challenged boy from our city, looking bewildered as a stream of fluid ran from his red nose, his face covered with patches of dry mud.

Mentally challenged people were allowed to roam the streets of our city, since there was no institution to take care of them. They were looked down upon and were the object of mockery and harassment by the people. They were beaten regularly and children often threw stones as they taunted them and called them horrible names.

I called out, "Hizo, did you escape from Saddam?"

As he looked my way, his eyes seemed cloudy and he seemed to be in a daze as he muttered the words he'd said hundreds of times every day: "Give me a quarter."

I told him that Iraqi money was now useless, but I reached out and handed him a few of the remaining almonds at the bottom of my bag.

Suddenly, I picked up the scent of grilled meat, mixed with the acrid smell of burning tires from somewhere nearby. I turned and started toward the source of the aroma. Soon I came across four young boys standing around a fire made from the tires of an abandoned vehicle. They were roasting the tiny featherless bodies of sparrows on sticks. One of the boys proudly told me that he had killed the sparrows with his slingshot. It would surely be a meager meal, but at least they would have something to eat that day. I decided to sit with them and let the warmth of the foul-smelling fire dry my wet jacket and pants.

As I sat, I asked about the boys' families. They told me they were all orphans who once lived in an orphanage in Duhok. The orphanage staff abandoned the facility at the first sign of danger, so the boys made their own escape plan and fled to the mountains.

One of the boys was pale and thin. I learned that his name was Mihvan. His father had been killed in the war and his mother had been forced to leave him at the orphanage because she was unable to take care of him. The other three boys had taken turns helping Mihvan walk toward the border over the course of four long, arduous days.

When the sparrows were well done and ready to eat, though covered with the soot from the tires, I was pleasantly surprised that the boys offered me a tiny drumstick. I thanked them and popped it into my mouth. I savored the needle-sized leg and thought it was the most delicious piece of meat I had ever tasted.

As we talked, I decided it would be impossible to find my family among the mass tangle of humanity, so I told the boys I would join them for the remaining four-hour hike to the border. Perhaps I would find my family there. The thought at least gave me some degree of hope. I'd cross the one mountain between the village and the border and then I'd see what the future had in store.

When the sparrows had all been eaten (which didn't take long), we joined the tens of thousands of people trudging up the steep, narrow trail along the rocky slope at the edge of Iraqi Kurdistan. It was a terrifying walk as we fought to maintain each foothold in the soft mud, sending loose stones hurtling down into the seemingly bottomless gorge.

The caravan of refugees stretched out for miles, like an endless line of migrating ants. There were harrowing moments of fear, combined with anger and disappointment. We also had to watch for stones falling from overhead, since the trail zigzagged across the ridge, doubling back on itself time after time.

After a while, it was my turn to carry Mihvan on my back. He was getting weaker by the moment and as I carried him, I could hear his faint whimpers of pain in my ears. Before long, I was exhausted and could barely hold myself upright. To bolster my own courage and strength, I began to sing an old Kurdish folksong softly. A few moments later, I noticed that Mihvan's moaning had stopped. I was secretly glad, since it allowed me to concentrate on simply putting one aching foot in front of the other.

A few meters further, I reached a point where I simply couldn't carry Mihvan another step. I eased to the side of the trail and leaned on a rock. I asked the boy nearest me to help me set Mihvan on the ground for a few moments. It was then that we discovered that Mihvan had died. We gathered around Mihvan's lifeless body, not knowing how to act. We knew we couldn't bury him on the side of the rocky slope. As we were debating what to do, an old man told us that the only thing we *could* do was cover Mihvan's face and leave him where he lay. After some discussion, we decided to carry Mihvan's body back to the village and give him a proper burial.

On the way back, it started to rain, which made the hike even more treacherous. We all fell several times on the slippery terrain, but we finally made it back to the village, where we then began to look around for a shovel. As the rain poured down, we managed to dig a hole barely large enough to contain Mihvan's body, but we knew it would have to do. We erected a makeshift gravestone and recited a last prayer for the poor boy, our tears mixing with the raindrops that slid down our sad faces.

With that task complete, we rejoined the line of refugees on the grueling trek toward the border. From time to time, people rushed behind the nearest rock to relieve themselves of the anguish caused by attacks of diarrhea. There was a constant background noise of crying babies in their mothers' arms. Many men and women carried huge packs of belongings, which became even heavier as the rain soaked everything in them. They would advance a few meters, then lean on a rock to catch their breath or sit down in exhaustion, looking through their packs to see what they could throw away to lighten their load.

A short way ahead, I saw an old man, his shaking legs threatening to buckle beneath the huge load on his back. He stopped and got rid of a few things, then rejoined the trek. Among the things he threw away was a box of matches, which I scooped up and shoved into my pocket.

Some fortunate families travelled with their belongings strapped onto the backs of mules. I had once heard about a Kurdish man who exchanged a brand new Mercedes for a mule. It was probably the best trade he ever made, since a mule was infinitely better suited for carrying a family's precious belongings over a slippery mountain pass.

It took more than four hours to reach the mountain peak, where I said goodbye to my young friends and began to search for my family. There were thousands of people blanketing the area, all waiting to cross the border into Turkey.

At that height there were no trees, except some scraggly bushes. Patches of snow cowered in the shadows of the mountainside. Nearly all of the thousands of refugees were trapped with no food and no blankets in freezing temperatures, running for their lives from the brutality of the Iraqi army, only to face slow death on the border.

I walked toward the border crossing to see if my family had already reached safety. The road was flooded with people, and though I received many kicks and shoves as I pushed my way through the crowd, I finally arrived at the crossing point. It was a three-meter wide muddy path, surrounded by minefields on both sides. About a hundred meters ahead, I saw a group of Turkish soldiers in military raincoats, ready to fire if ordered to do so. On the Kurdish side of the border were thousands of desperate people waiting to cross amid harsh conditions.

The border had been sealed off and the Turkish army was trying to force the Kurds back to their own side. Suddenly, the mountainside was rocked by the thunder of Iraqi artillery fire. As the refugees at the front of the line panicked and surged forward, the Turkish soldiers opened fire. I fell on my stomach in the soft mud and hugged the ground until the shooting stopped. Then I slowly lifted myself up and looked around.

"You killed my daughter!" A nearby woman screamed. "We escaped from Saddam, just to be killed by you!"

We were trapped between the two mightiest armies of the Middle East and there seemed to be no way to escape. Realizing I wasn't going to get across the border, I went back up the mountainside to resume my search for my family. As I walked, I overheard a Kurdish man and wife bickering. She told her husband she was cold and wet and needed some sleep. He countered sarcastically that maybe she should retire to her warm feather bed in the crusted mud and he would follow her shortly. She growled that the last thing she needed at that moment was to listen to his sarcasm.

The cold rain continued to fall, making my body shiver and shake like an Egyptian belly dancer. Finally, the couple stopped arguing and fell into a dismal silence for a long moment. Then the man lying in the mud raised his head and thrust his hands up toward the sky in a protesting gesture.

As the raindrops hit his desperate face and angry eyes, he shouted, "God, why don't you stop this rain? Can't you see we're dying down here? Or, like Bush, have you made a pact with Saddam and will get a share of his oil for letting him massacre us?"

In the midst of the desperate situation, the air was suddenly filled with angry voices, shouting curses. Two names frequently heard among those curses were George Bush and Saddam Hussein.

After a long time of searching among the crowd, I finally stumbled upon one of my relatives. He told me my family was there. To my great relief, he confirmed that they were all still alive. He led me to them and we had a joyous reunion in the midst of a terrible situation. I hugged my mother, sisters, and brothers. My father asked me about the goats. I told him I'd left the goats in the Mangish village in the care of a clergyman, who had promised to take care of them until our return.

Hearing the news, my father shouted, "Can't you ever do anything right?"

Something inside me wanted to shout back, "Father, people are leaving their children at the side of the road to freeze to death because they can't carry them any longer—yet you expect me to bring seven goats safely to the border?"

My father was a hardworking man who had spent all his life trying to provide for seven sons and six daughters, but my relationship with him had always been stormy and full of turbulence. I was never able to satisfy him, no matter how hard I tried. I never heard a word of praise from him. He constantly told me I was a failure and that my cousin was much better than I was.

Whenever I'd start wondering about why he treated me that way, I'd remember a story he used to tell me about his own father. When he was fourteen, his father had told him, "Son, you're fourteen now, which makes you a mature man. It's time to sell the sheep, so which would you rather have—a wife or a gun?"

My father had replied without any hesitation, "A gun, Dad."

His father's eyes shone with pride at his son's choice. Now he had a man he could depend on. His father bought him a rifle and took him into the mountains to teach him the art of warfare.

They say that it's common in Kurdish society for fathers to push their eldest sons hard—right to the edge—to help them to grow up before their time and be ready to take over the family's responsibilities. A father might come home one evening, ask his wife to put some bread in a hand-woven bag, and then take his rifle from the wall and announce that it was time to go.

The wife wouldn't ask any questions. She would wait until her husband was gone to shed her bitter tears. Sometimes it would take years for the husband to return—and oftentimes he never came back. The family would receive only his blood-stained Kurdish turban, a sign that he had been killed defending the land.

My extended family was large—thirty-five members—and like everyone around us at the border, we were starving. We had to get some food, because only God knew when the Turks would finally open the border. I told my family I had seen huge piles of food along the trail that people had thrown away as they lightened their packs, thinking that the border crossing would be quick. We decided that all the male members of the family would go back down the trail to look for supplies, but we knew we'd have to hurry because there were many other people who had come to the same conclusion.

As I walked down, the last one in the family march, I saw a man coming up the trail with two sacks of food. I asked if there was still food along the trail, and he said there was, but many people were already fighting over the abandoned supplies.

A short distance farther, I saw a man carrying a white bag on his back, struggling up the narrow trail. He stopped, dropped the bag, and raced behind the nearest rock to relieve his diarrhea. I ran toward the bag and found that it was full of rice. I threw it across my back and headed back toward my family as fast as I could go.

Twenty minutes later, I was approaching my family, announcing that I had found some rice. It brought smiles to everyone and the children immediately began looking for firewood while my mother and my uncle's wife started piling stones to serve as a stove. They found an old dusty oilcan that could be used as a cooking pan and filled it with rainwater. The problem was that all the sticks we found were rain drenched and refused to catch fire. Then I remembered I had seen lots of ammunition along the trail, tossed aside to lighten people's loads. I took all the children with me to collect bullets.

Back at our little camp, we removed the bullet heads by hammering them with rocks. Then we dumped out the gunpowder. Adding that to the bottom of the pile in our makeshift stove allowed us to get the fire started. I blew on the fire so much that the smoke billowing up from the soggy pile of sticks painted my face black and my eyes brimmed with tears. Finally, the rice began to cook, and after what seemed like an eternity, we had a meal. It was only rice, boiled in a muddy oilcan filled with rainwater, but it was a delicious meal. We made sure that not a single grain of rice was wasted.

A short time later, I saw the men of the family moving slowly toward us, carrying sacks of food on their backs. I hurried to help my father, whose legs were trembling under his heavy load. They had managed to gather enough supplies to feed the family for several days.

As mother told my father about my heroic deed, bringing rice back so quickly, he looked at me suspiciously. It was at least a four-hour round trip to find food and bring it back, yet I had only been gone twenty minutes. I explained in a shaky voice that I had run into a person I had known in school who had generously shared a half-bag of rice with me. My father may have had doubts about my story, but he said nothing and let the issue drop.

The weather deteriorated even further, and more and more children and elderly people died. I thought about the absurdity of all that waiting—waiting for the rain to stop, waiting for the Turks to finally show mercy, waiting for the Iraqi army to slaughter our people, waiting for slow death on the top of a mountain. It was surreal—and it all seemed so futile.

My romantic image of rain was shattered and I now saw it as a harbinger of death to hundreds of infants, children, and old people. I found myself silently begging the sky to stop the rain and make the sun come back.

The next afternoon, my fourteen-year-old brother, Shirko, shouted at our mother as he threw clothes onto the muddy ground, blaming her for not bringing his brand new jeans with her as they fled the city. He stopped shouting when I grabbed him by the neck and growled, "You leave Mother alone! She's already had more than she can take. Don't you realize what's happening here? People are dying from cold and starvation, but you're whining about a stupid pair of jeans!"

Shirko quieted down and retreated without another word, but my cousins teased him, saying an Iraqi soldier was probably walking around in his new jeans at that moment.

Since there weren't enough blankets or tarps for everyone, many men slept on the cold, muddy ground near to women and children who shivered together under plastic sheets supported by four barely fixed sticks. The tarps covered only a small portion of their bodies. Most of their bodies were still exposed to the elements. The rainwater gathered on the roofs of the tarps until it grew too heavy, at which time the tarps collapsed, sending water down onto the already shivering women and children. Then they would stretch the sheets out again and crawl back underneath, praying the rain would finally end.

Our family had no plastic tarps, so we fixed two blankets, under which huddled the women and youngest children while the men and boys stayed in the open all day and night. Sometimes we burned a few things to generate at least a little heat during the night. As the night grew darker, only two sounds lulled us to sleep—the dripping of the rain and the crying of babies.

Except for brief intervals, the rain continued for three days and nights as we waited for the Turks to let us cross the border. Hundreds of thousands of people now inhabited the area, waiting for one of three things: to die from cold and hunger, to be slaughtered by the Iraqi army, or to be blown up by a mine while collecting wood for heat or snow for water.

My second cousin had been married only two days before we fled our city. The unfortunate newlyweds had to spend their honeymoon with us on the mountain. His bride had been tossed into the overcrowded Hotel Wet Blanket with twenty other women and children. They stole furtive looks from each other, obviously wishing they could be together, but Kurdish married couples never hugged or kissed in the presence of other people.

At dawn, after another cold and miserable night, I heard the screams of my sister from the blanket shelter. I hurried toward the cries, but was driven back by my mother. My sister was giving birth to a baby! The women and children stood in a small circle around my sister to give her some privacy. Finally, there was a tiny cry as an infant refugee entered the world. It was the first time I had seen anyone smile since our ordeal began—although I did notice that my sister's mother-in-law was disappointed when she learned that the baby was a girl.

As I talked with my first cousin (my sister's husband) about names for the baby, suggesting the name Hivi (which means "hope" in Kurdish), we heard screams of anguish from the blanket shelter: The baby had died. We knew we'd have to wait to give her a proper burial. There was no place on the mountainside that wasn't already occupied and we had no means to dig a grave.

Even so, we decided to try to lay the poor child to rest as best we could. Using our hands, sharp stones, and pocket-knives, we finally managed to scoop out a tiny grave in the rocky earth. My mother then handed the baby, wrapped in a small piece of white cloth, to my first cousin, who tenderly lowered the tiny body into the hole. His eyes glistened with tears, which he made a huge effort to control, since Kurdish men were not supposed to cry. As for me, I felt a tear roll down my cheek before I could wipe it away.

Life was such a bundle of contradictions—filled with laughter and tears. While we were in tears, I had a vision of the baby's face smiling as she winged up from the mountain height, the closest it would ever get to angels in heaven. In the pale moonlight, across the horizon, loomed the Kurdish Mount Ararat, the place where Noah's Ark had landed after the Great Flood. The history of Mesopotamia had led to the belief that Kurdish land was part of God's paradise on Earth.

It was the first time the hand of death had wrapped its icy fingers around our family. I began to worry about Younis, my two-year-old brother. I loved him dearly and was afraid I would lose him. I shivered at the thought of seeing him lowered into a grave in the middle of nowhere. I put extra clothes on him to try to keep him warm, until he looked like an overstuffed doll. I took him under my jacket to warm him with my own body and rubbed his rosy little hands to keep them from freezing. When we had a fire, I brought him close—so close that his little eyes filled with tears from the smoke. On one occasion, the fire singed bangs of his blond hair.

One afternoon, there was a huge turmoil among the people as they heard on the radio that the Turkish government, under pressure from the international community, would soon open the border. Our family, along with thousands of other refugees, pushed toward the crossing point, but as the refugees tried to cross, Turkish soldiers fired into the air above the crowd. Women and children started throwing stones at the soldiers, but they continued firing, causing the crowd to back up—some of them stepping into the minefields, where they were blown to pieces.

I rushed through the crowd to see what had happened, ignoring my mother's shouts to stay close to the family. Bodies lay on the ground a short distance from the border. Many others stood frozen in place as they realized they were trapped in a minefield.

Women and children screamed as they saw their loved ones killed needlessly. One woman tried desperately to run into the minefield to help her son, who was standing paralyzed in the minefield, afraid to move in any direction, but her husband and several other men prevented her from rushing to her own death.

Several brave men with military experience extracted mines using only knives as they made their way to wounded or stranded people in the minefields. They rescued as many as they could, but also brought back dead bodies wrapped in blood-stained blankets. I knew one of those men personally. His name was Umrow and he would later tell me that he had managed to extract some 300 mines. It was impossible to estimate how many lives Umrow saved through his efforts and those of his courageous comrades.

As a huge wave of people poured across the border, the rain again began to fall, causing the Turkish soldiers to withdraw to their bunkers on the hilltop and allow people to cross freely. The next destination was a Kurdish village on the Turkish side of the border (called Dashtan in Kurdish and Uzumlu in Turkish). In some places, the borderline divided the Kurdish village into two halves, each half in a different nation. Sometimes cousins from the same village went to different schools—some to Turkish schools to learn Turkish and become "Mountain Turks," and some to attend Iraqi schools to learn Arabic and become part of the Arab world. It had been that way for hundreds of years. When the Arabs, Turks, or Persians needed Kurds to fight in their wars, they saw the Kurds as brothers living together in one land. However, when the Kurds cried for freedom, they were considered outlaws to be annihilated and buried in mass graves in the desert sand.

The situation on the Turkish side of the border was no better than on the Kurdish side, but at least we felt safe from Iraqi army raids. My exhausted family walked around, looking for a place to settle before sunset. Finally, my father saw a group of trees in the foothills and urged us to move toward them before another family could lay claim to them. Within minutes, we were tightening a wet blanket between the trees and wrapping the sides with two more. As we worked, we discovered we had camped in an old graveyard, but it made no difference. The women and children quickly huddled inside the makeshift shelter as the men and older boys stood outside. We knew we would have to survive on the few scraps of food we had managed to bring with us.

As night fell, a cold wind blew through the wet blankets, making it even colder inside the shelter. I worried that we would lose several of the younger children, including Younis. In our religion, it is strictly forbidden to cut down trees in a graveyard, since it is believed that the souls of pious dead men would curse us if we did. My cousin and I climbed the oak trees and dangled from branches so the other men could break them off and burn them. I didn't worry about being cursed. I decided the souls of the pious dead would not want to come out in such terrible weather only to curse some miserable refugees.

We finally managed to get a fire started, then huddled around it as close as we could, but there wasn't enough room for everyone. I found an empty can, filled it with glowing coals from the fire, and took it into the shelter to give the women and children some heat. When I returned, I had lost my position close to the fire, so I curled up on the ground in a fetal position to survive the night.

A few minutes later, my mother screamed in panic, "Soleen is dead!"

My cousin came rushing outside, carrying my young sister, then started shaking her and slapping her face. My father then came hurrying out of the shelter with the can of coals, shouting for everyone to get back outside quickly. A short time later, Soleen began to cough and regain consciousness. She had been suffocated by carbon monoxide from the glowing coals. I was stunned. I had only wanted to help them survive the night, but I had nearly caused the death of my sister.

As the light of dawn approached, a sea of white and blue plastic tarps stretched to the horizon. There were nearly a quarter million refugees in the area. The refugees from the Dashtan (Uzumlu) camp were virtually all from our city. Most of them were Kurds, but they also included Assyrian Christians and Iraqi army deserters.

The flood of refugees into Turkey had been so sudden that no international humanitarian aid was yet available in this forgotten part of the world—no tents and no food supplies. The only source of water was the snow that clung to the rocky hills several hundred meters above the ridge. Women had to crawl for two hours to bring back snow-melted water. Hundreds of people died each day, especially the elderly, infants, and young children, from malnutrition, disease, and exposure.

Kurds in southeast Turkey heard about our ordeal and launched a private humanitarian aid campaign manned by hundreds of volunteers. Trucks began to arrive carrying food, blankets, and warm clothes, but it wasn't nearly enough to help the massive number of refugees. At the sight of an aid truck, waves of starving and cold-stricken refugees stormed the vehicle, pushing and fighting to get a piece of bread, a can of food, or a blanket.

One day, I managed to jump up onto one of the trucks, but I was quickly thrown off and came up empty-handed. Moments later, I saw a loaf of brown Turkish bread fly out of the hands of two young refugees who were quarreling over it on top of the truck. I jumped as high as I could and snatched it, then ran away as fast as I could before someone else could grab it out of my hand. On my way back "home," I couldn't resist the temptation of the brown Turkish bread. I took a big bite, then handed the remaining loaf to my mother.

A number of non-governmental relief agencies arrived at the camp and attempted to get food and emergency supplies to us, but they faced tremendous logistics problems because of the huge number of refugees and the difficult terrain. Members of the international press corps had also arrived and were broadcasting reports from the camp.

My father went back to his old habit of listening to news on his pocket-sized radio. He told me our situation had caused outrage in some Western countries. The American Secretary of

State, James Baker, was scheduled to visit Turkey the next day and would probably make a stop at several refugee camps.

For the first time in three weeks, I thought about taking a bath. It would involve a two-hour trek down the mountain to a frigid little stream, since the water came from melted snow on the mountains above, but if James Baker was going to visit, I wanted to be his interpreter. Later, I was disappointed to learn that Baker had visited a bigger camp in Chukurjia, a few kilometers from ours.

The next day, I joined the crowd storming a Turkish relief truck but was driven back by Turkish soldiers firing into the air. I sat on the ground and waited, in the hope that I'd be able to bring something back for my family before sunset.

Then I saw two foreigners with a TV camera. I approached them and found out they were from the BBC. One of them introduced himself as Jeremy Bowen, the BBC's Middle East correspondent. They asked if they could interview me about the exodus and the conditions in the camp. After the interview, they asked if they could hire me as an interpreter, and I happily agreed.

As we toured the camp, they broadcasted horrific images. A pale woman surrounded by shivering children lay under a plastic tarp. She had given birth to a dead baby son the night before. His grandfather carried him to a small village mosque for a last prayer in preparation for burial. We went to the mosque but we couldn't find the grandfather. He had already taken the infant to the cemetery.

Dead bodies wrapped in dirty pieces of cloth lined the ground close to the mosque wall, awaiting last prayers from a Muslim clergyman who was mumbling them as fast as he could. The clergyman told us he was saying prayers for more than sixty dead people every day.

We went to the cemetery and found the grandfather sitting next to a partially dug grave. As he wiped a tear from his white beard, he told us it was the second grandson he had buried that week.

Shortly thereafter, we saw mourners carrying the body of a man who had died while collecting firewood on the mountainside. He had been blown up by a mine, one of thousands of hidden instruments of death that claimed innocent lives daily.

Hundreds of fresh graves filled the cemetery. Most of the dead were children, elderly people, victims of typhoid, dehydration, and hunger, but others had been killed by mines or in skirmishes over food supplies. Nearly every fifteen minutes, women screamed and pulled their hair as they walked behind a group of men carrying a dead body to the cemetery.

At the end of the day, Jeremy put something in my hand. When I opened my palm, I saw a crisp, green one-hundred dollar bill. It was the first time in my life I'd seen such a large amount of money.

On my way back to my family, I saw American Hercules planes circling above the camp. Soon they dropped supplies tied to beautifully colored parachutes over the foothills south of the camp. Thousands of people raced toward the parachutes and I joined the marathon, running as fast as I could. As I drew closer to the landing area, there were two explosions and people froze in their tracks. Most of the supplies had landed in a minefield. Unaware of the danger, three young people lost their lives that day.

I quickly headed in another direction where I had seen a few parachutes go down. When I arrived, there were already some 200 people around each package, tearing it apart with knives and axes. It seemed mission impossible for me to get my hands close to any of the packages. I knew if I fell down while trying to get a share of the bounty, I'd be crushed under the stampeding mob. However, I was as desperate as any of the others, so I pushed forward and reached through the hoard of human bodies and felt my hand touch something. I curled my fingers around it and pulled with all my might. To my surprise, it was a green American army camouflage jacket. I threw the jacket on so no one could rip it from my hands. Then, wearing my new jacket, I turned and went back to my family. When I returned, I took off the jacket and gave it to my father.

The first thing I asked Jeremy the next day was if he could mention in his next report that the Americans were dropping supplies into minefields and thereby accidentally killing refugees as they rushed to receive them. Jeremy agreed and the next day the Americans dropped packages closer to the camp. Unfortunately, even that caused an accidental death a couple of days later. One of the packages landed on a hillside and dislodged a big rock, which then rolled down the hill and crushed a woman who was sitting near her makeshift stove and cooking lunch for her children.

As more journalists arrived at the refugee camps, I gained a reputation as a reliable interpreter and made even more money. Supplies continued to be dropped on a regular basis, including blankets, tents, clothes, and military food packages containing ready-to-eat meals (MRE). As the days went by, things got a little better, but thousands of refugees were still sleeping in the crusted mud.

Hygiene was also a big concern since we lacked drinking water, adequate heat, and proper sanitation facilities. Diarrhea swept through the camp. If you needed to answer nature's call, you had to walk at least half an hour in any direction to reach the outskirts of the camp. Many of the elderly, sick, and very young couldn't walk such a distance, so they had no choice but to relieve themselves wherever they were.

Turkish army doctors helped as many patients as they could, but they could only help those who could get into the heavily guarded army base. Non-government organizations, such as Doctors Without Borders (Médecins Sans Frontières, MSF) set up temporary clinics consisting of a couple of tents—one for minor treatment and the other for more severe cases. They also made arrangements to transfer seriously ill patients to a hospital in Hakary. A few doctors and nurses worked nearly around the clock, but they were terribly short of medicine and sometimes the huge crowd waiting outside the tents was simply too much for them to handle.

Once I was walking into the MSF tent when an old Kurdish man was struggling to make a French doctor understand that he had severe diarrhea. He put his hand into his mouth as if he were eating, then moved his hand quickly to his bottom. He raised both hands to tell the doctor that he was having bowel movements at least ten times a day.

As if there weren't enough pollution from human waste, refugees caught Iraqi Arab men—sent by Iraqi security authorities—dropping chemicals into water sources.

One night, I was sleeping on my side, shivering from the cold under the jacket I used to cover my head and shoulders, when I heard people making noise. I lifted the edge of my muddy jacket and opened my left eye, my head lying on the pair of stolen shoes I was using as a pillow. I could see feet in military boots moving past. I was too sleepy to wake up fully, though I expected to receive a kick from a boot or a blow from a rifle butt at any minute, since that was the normal procedure when Turkish soldiers wanted us to do something. However, I was surprised when I felt a gentle touch on my shoulder.

I poked my head out and saw an American soldier. He spoke to me, gesturing to help me understand that I had to move since they wanted to dig a hole where I was lying.

I replied in English, "Are you going to set up sanitation facilities? That's a high priority here."

Looking at my filthy clothes and my greasy hair, he shouted, "Hey, captain! Over here! There's a guy who speaks English better than I do!"

As I spoke with the Americans, they asked if I'd work for them, and I readily agreed.

People soon started to wake up, but they looked warily at the newcomers in military uniforms holding shovels in their hands. They might have fallen from the sky during the night, since they hadn't been there the day before.

Finally, I heard one of the refugees say, "Shame on us. They're building toilets for us and we're just standing around watching."

With that, a group of Kurdish men moved forward and began to help the American soldiers. The atmosphere was friendly as the soldiers socialized with the refugees while they worked—

under the curious gaze of the Turkish soldiers. The arrival of the American troops was a huge relief to the refugees, since the Turkish army occasionally treated people savagely.

Coming back with my first MRE box, I saw an old man in filthy white Kurdish pants. He was crying in agony while making his mess among the throng since he couldn't walk to the outskirts of the camp. His lips were cracked from severe dehydration and he was trembling from the cold. As I approached, he told me in a weak voice that he wanted to die. He wondered why he was still alive while the angel of death was reaping the lives of young children all around him. He hadn't eaten or drunk anything since the previous day. Then he raised his shaking hands and prayed for God to take him, hoping death would end his torture.

I sat beside him and unpacked my MRE box. I opened a pack of soup and began feeding it to him with a plastic spoon. Then I gave him some peach-flavored drink and finished his meal with a piece of strawberry cake.

When he was done, he smiled gratefully and said, "Thanks, son. That was delicious meat. What was it?"

I told him it was an American food called ham—part of a pig. He recoiled in horror and cried, "Oh, Great Allah! I've eaten pig meat! Gracious Allah, forgive me! I've sinned and I'll go hell for that!"

I tried to comfort the old man, saying, "Take it easy! Allah loves you. This food was dropped to you from the sky so you could stay alive—and I don't think hell could be much worse than here."

The American troops shared a Turkish military bunker on the hilltop to coordinate the relief work and bring some order to the camp. The next day, I went northwest of the camp with a group of American soldiers to install a piping system for drinking-water from a stream a few hundred meters up in the foothills. We were staggering up in military formation, carrying plastic pipes and other equipment on our shoulders, when I heard a blast at the front of the formation.

I fell to the ground and the plastic pipes rolled down the cliffside. As I started to get up, a soldier shouted, "Medic! Soldier down!"

Then a group of men carried a wounded soldier passed me. An American soldier lost one of his legs in a mine accident that day.

The Turkish military headquarters was off limits to refugees, and though I could go inside with American escort, I couldn't enter alone. One day, I received an urgent call of nature, so I rushed through the gate, but I was met by a Turkish soldier, who knocked me down and shoved the barrel of his rifle into my temple.

A Turkish officer saved my life by shouting, "American! American!"

Despite the pain, I was relieved to have survived, especially since Turkish soldiers had bashed in the head of another boy who had rushed through the gate to try to reach the Turkish military doctor for his dying mother.

One day, while I was walking out of the MSF medical tent, I stumbled upon one of my childhood friends, Majo. After a warm handshake, I saw that he was the same guy I had always known. His clothes were clean and his hair jelled, as if he were going to a job interview and not a miserable refugee. I asked if he needed any translation help with the doctor, but Majo didn't need medical attention. He was there because many girls came to the tent with their sick younger brothers and sisters.

I asked if he helped his family to get food, but he told me his brothers took care of that. He used the relief trucks and parachute drops mainly as ways to press his body against women struggling to grab something for their hungry families. If he managed to grab something himself, he generally used it as an excuse to hook up with a woman.

He had been a girl addict when we were in Duhok too. His nickname was "Glue", because if he met a girl in the bazaar, he'd spend the next three or four hours following her to every corner of the market and into every shop. He made sure she was in his sights until she finished her shopping, then he'd follow her all the way to her house, where he'd spend days walking around her alley in the afternoons in the hope that he might be able to date her.

I thought the terrible conditions of the camp would have curtailed Majo's appetite for girls. They looked like witches with their filthy clothes and filthy hair, and most of them hadn't taken a bath in more than a month. He told me that the girls had become even more attractive to him now that they looked sexy and wild.

Then he added, "They're also not thrown behind locked doors, as used to be the case all the time. There are thousands of girls, all in the open, with no walls and no curtains. We're all one big family here. The fathers and mothers have many other worries than to watch out for their daughters."

As Majo was speaking, I remembered the saying, "Some people's adversity is other people's prosperity." In the midst of a disastrous situation, with death and disease everywhere,

Majo was walking around in his elegant clothes, chasing women for a nightly rendezvous.

He told me he enjoyed following girls as they made the two-hour trek up the mountain to get some snow for cooking and drinking. However, he did admit that he'd had a difficult encounter a few days earlier. The woman he was following got annoyed and turned back several times to tell him to leave her alone.

But Majo kept following her, showing his admiration by saying things like, "You're asking me to leave you alone, but how can a man leave his soul? You're my soul, and without you I'm just a wretched body."

Finally, she asked, "Just what do you want from me?"

He replied, "I want to spend every minute of the rest of my life with you. I want to come to your tent and ask for your hand, so you'll know how serious I am."

"Oh really?" said the girl.

She then asked him to follow her to her plastic tarp. She also asked him to help her carry the metal can filled with snow water, which he did happily, excited that the girl had fallen into his trap. He struggled under the heavy can balanced on his shoulder, which shook at times, sending freezing water onto his head and shoulders.

As they drew near the plastic tarp, she took the water can and asked him to wait for her signal. As he waited, his fantasies of an imminent romantic encounter ran wild. After a few minutes, she poked her head from behind the tarp and waved for him to come over. His adrenaline pumping, Majo rushed toward the tarp, where he was caught by the collar and dragged under the tarp. He found himself surrounded by three men with big black moustaches and thick wooden logs in their hands. The men knocked him down and beat him mercilessly. His begging for forgiveness was useless as the hammering continued. He shouted that he had honest intentions and wanted to propose marriage.

Finally, one of the men growled, "Marriage? You shameless and ill-mannered man—that woman is my wife."

With that, they threw him out from under the tarp, bruised but still alive.

One of my sisters, who had joined in our escape with her three children, was an extra burden for us. Her husband had been forced into military service as a soldier in the Iraqi army during the Gulf War in southern Iraq. She had run into the mountains in fear of persecution from the same army that her husband was fighting for as a soldier.

Hearing the news about his family's fate, her husband deserted his army unit in Basra and started a hazardous trip to the Turkish border in search of them. To reach the northern border, he had to avoid the rebels of a newly erupted uprising in the south, the Iraqi army republican guards, as well as the constant Allied forces air strikes. After a long search, he managed to join us in our camp. He told us that Duhok was a ghost town—except for an occasional stray cat or dog.

The horrendous footage broadcast by TV reporters caused outrage all over the world. The international community voted to create a temporary safe haven to allow for the return of the refugees. The Americans in the camp urged us to return to our hometowns in Iraq, putting a halt to our miserable two-month sojourn. Finally, we would have a chance to return home, but there was—and still is—the fear of a future exodus.

We were keen to return to our homes, even though we had heard that Iraqi soldiers had pillaged most of the houses and razed entire neighborhoods to the ground. But we made it clear that we wouldn't agree to the return unless the Iraqi army and the secret police withdrew from our territory. We demanded that coalition forces provide protection and emergency relief for the returning refugees.

Joy prevailed in the camp and, clutching their belongings, people headed back to their homes. However, we were returning from a war, with every second family having lost at least one family member in a refugee camp or along the road on the Iraqi side of the border.

Our family was also excited about returning home. We unfastened the tents and packed our possessions, never even considering the American transition tent camp that had been set up in Silopi to help returning refugees.

I ran to the Turkish border police headquarters to bid goodbye to the American soldiers I had worked with, but they suggested that I wait and leave in a cattle truck to Silopi. They even suggested the possibility of taking me back to America to get a chance of a new life.

I sat on a nearby rock and imagined myself in a cowboy hat, riding a horse with a beautiful blonde American girl with the nose of Sandra Bullock, the smile of Julia Roberts, and the lips of Angelina Jolie riding beside me. Then I thought about my sweetheart, Pari, with her black eyes and long black hair. I hoped that one day all the suffering would end and we could go back to college, where I wouldn't wait a single day to tell her how much she meant to me.

Then I saw the snowy Kurdish mountain peaks and the thousands of white tents stretching across the foothills. I smiled as I remembered an old saying about the Kurdish people. They spend all their lives on the move, and even after dying they go neither to hell nor heaven. Instead, their souls spend eternity as refugees in worn-out tents between the two worlds.

At that moment, I said to myself, "*I've had enough of tents*".

I might end up as a success story, working hard in the land of opportunity to achieve the American dream. But the question that haunted me at that moment was, could I move out of this hell without hurting other people? Like what Tom said referring to the magician's coffin trick in *The Glass Menagerie*, "Can I come out of the coffin without moving any nails?

Could I leave the love of my life without letting her know how I felt about her? I decided I'd go back to my sweetheart. I would sacrifice anything in the world to see her heavenly smile again.

I went back to my family's tent and was told they were all ready to go, but I had to carry something. I chose two boxes of American MREs. We headed to the crowded border pass, with extracted mines heaped on both sides. When we reached the place where we had camped before the crossing, my sister dropped the load on her back and ran to the tiny grave of her baby daughter. She mumbled some prayers with tears coming down her cheeks, kissed the gravestone, and bid a last farewell before leaving, probably forever.

After a three-hour walk to the first Kurdish village on the Iraqi side, we managed to find some transportation to take us to Duhok. A group of boys sat in the rear of the pickup, singing and saluting when passing coalition forces. The sight of those soldiers gave us a sense of security. In the city, buildings had been bombed, neighborhoods demolished, electrical and telephone wires downed. Some of the intersections were blocked by abandoned cars and trucks with smashed fenders and bullet holes in the windows. The Iraqi army had been pushed south, away from the Kurdish area, but army helmets and military boots were still scattered on the sidewalks. We arrived in our neighborhood and saw that most of the doors were broken, with pieces of furniture and belongings scattered on the roads.

Soldiers and people from the southern towns had cleaned out most of the houses and shops. Our house had been looted. My mother sat in the middle of the empty house and cried. Everything was gone, including the blue carpet that had been a wedding gift from her mother. I rushed upstairs to my room, but nothing was there except my books, scattered on the floor. I'd put Pari's picture between the pages of Victor Hugo's novel *Toilers of the Sea*. I searched the piles of books until I found the photo, then stuffed it in my shirt pocket and went back downstairs.

My mother was still crying, but my father said, "Stop it, woman. We should be thanking God that we all came back alive." I smiled as my father put his hand on my mother's shoulder and said as he helped her to her feet, "One day, all this will end."

There was no electricity, no water, and a shortage of food, but the fear of the unknown was the most difficult thing to deal with. After a few days of acclimatization to civilization, I headed to Mosul, where my college was located.

Since I had to go through Iraqi government territory, I was worried. I had appeared in some Western TV reports and had been warned by a correspondent to "think twice before going back to Iraq. Saddam's eyes are everywhere."

It didn't matter. I was determined to see Pari, even if I died in the attempt. I went straight into the class and shook hands with the few others who had also returned. I sat in class with my eyes fixed on the half-open door, hoping my sweetheart would emerge.

As time passed, more students appeared, but I grew more worried with each new face. I was greatly relieved when I met Sazan walking down the corridor. I can't remember if I said hello to her or asked her if her family was okay. I only remember asking if Pari was all right. Sazan smiled wearily and told me that after fleeing to a refugee camp in Iran, Pari and her family had emigrated to the United States. After Sazan left, I sat alone, my face buried in my hands.

I picked up a nail and carved these words on Pari's desk: "I will love you for eternity."

My heart was broken into a million pieces. I'd have to suffer alone and bleed in pain as I tried to collect the pieces again. I tried to imagine life without Pari, and I found death more tempting.

But love is a power that should give meaning to our existence—not lead to our ruin. Once again, I had to emerge from the shadows and pick up the wreckage of my life. I had changed so much over the past few years that I had lost all concept of who I was. A part of me was gone—perhaps forever—and my only option was to begin searching for my other half again.

When Mountains Weep

When Mountains Weep

My father died in 2000, before hearing his long-awaited broadcast on the radio: "Saddam Hussein has been taken down." He didn't live to see the day when "all this will end."

Rasho was killed fighting in the Iraq-Iran War in 1987.

Simko Harky died in 1994, still clinging to his radio in the hope of a cure for his cancer.

Pari is a happily married woman with two children, living somewhere in the United States.

I never met Pari again, but I am a happily married man with a few more children, still living in Kurdistan, in the hope that *I* will someday have an opportunity to say what my father never got to say: "This is the day when all of this ends."